P9-DZM-251

BEYOND THE BROKEN HEART
A Journey Through Grief

CONTENTS

INTRODUCTION

On a beach vacation in January, 2004, I sat on a beautiful chaise one afternoon, reading a book as warm sunlight streamed into the room. The steady cadence of ocean waves accompanied the rhythm of a soft tropical breeze. I was at peace; life in that moment was carefree and full of contentment. My beloved husband, Leighton, sat in the next room, resting and relaxing. Our life together seemed perfect, complete in every way—not because we were on holiday, but because we were married and had each other to love and cherish.

Three months later Leighton was diagnosed with pancreatic cancer, an overwhelmingly terminal disease. Ninety days later he was dead. When he died, I was destroyed: my heart broke into one million small pieces. At fifty-five I was young and very old. I was too old to be young and too young to be old. I was suddenly very much alone.

So powerful was the experience of his illness and death that, for a while, I was certain I would die of a broken heart. Far beyond the poetic, I understood those souls portrayed in literature who languish with no will to live, slowly dying from insurmountable emotional loss. Cause of death: a broken heart. Though my soul survived largely intact, I found myself in frightening, unfamiliar spiritual territory. As I sat alone a few days after Leighton died, immobilized by shock, a tidal wave of emotion engulfed my entire being. I came face to face with the inescapable reality of grief.

There was no other name for that indescribable sense of helplessness, the utter hopelessness that threatened to overwhelm me completely. From deep within I knew that I must go through grief. I could not avoid it, delay it, deny it, or circumvent it. I sensed that grief would be both power and presence in my life for the unforeseeable future. And so began my own personal journey through grief.

Like you, I have faced death in the first person. Although I am not a therapist or professional, I have endeavored to fully understand my life-altering encounter with death and grief. Over many months I worked at grief, I read about grief, I strained to understand grief. Its compelling urgency became my relentless companion.

In my quest to understand grief, I discovered that we grieve because we love. In fact, the more we love, the greater our grief. The ratio of love to loss depends only on the depth of relationship measured by the quality of love. You might say that we grieve in direct proportion to the depth of our love. Few of us would forego love to avoid the pain of grief. Even in the face of grief we give thanks for having loved so deeply that when death touches our lives, we do nothing for a while except grieve.

We all have a story. "We spend our years as a tale that is told" (Psalm 90:9 KJV). A central part of your personal story is the chapter you continue to write through grief, a story you long to tell so that others will understand this pivotal moment in your life when, for you, all the world changed forever. Being able to share your story within the sanctity of a group of people who know the experience of death and grief helps you to realize that you are not alone. You are certain that you are heard and understood.

Herein lies the purpose of *Beyond the Broken Heart*. Within the sanctity of your group, you will find a community that shares your emotional isolation and loneliness. Together you will find support and encouragement as you seek a life of renewed hope and joy after your personal experience of grief. In the weeks to come, you will experience personal and spiritual growth and enrichment that will transform your grief as your broken heart is healed by God's triumphant adequacy. "He heals the brokenhearted, and binds up their wounds" (Psalm 147:3 NRSV). You also will discover that death has redemptive value as loss and survival inspire you to greater compassion for the suffering of others.

Each chapter combines stories from my own journey through grief and explores relevant topics using passages from the Bible to illustrate the unfamiliar emotions and questions of grief. You will find that the book explains both the spiritual and practical issues of grief and suggests specific strategies to guide you back to fullness of life. It is recommended that you read one chapter each week prior to your group session (the two supplemental chapters may be read if or when your group chooses to schedule those sessions).

The questions and prompts for personal reflection found throughout the book are provided to help you process your thoughts along your journey through grief. They are private and for your use only. You may want to share your thoughts and feelings with the group, or you may choose to be an active listener. Your participation is strictly voluntary. The group will respect the privacy and individuality of each participant's unique experience of grief.

Even as I will always cherish my marriage to Leighton, which was the best part of my life, I will continue to transform my experience of grief into a new life that honors the memory of my beloved husband, a life lived in gratitude for the steadfast love and faithfulness of God. This is the goal of your journey through grief as well: transformation and new life. As you embark upon this journey, may the promises of the Bible and the support of those who accompany you along the way sustain and encourage you to trust in life and contemplate hope. You are not alone.

Julie Yarbrough
Dallas, Texas

1
NAMING GRIEF

1
NAMING GRIEF

I sat impotently by his side, observing a beloved life fading away. Sunrise and sunset marked his last day of life upon the earth as slowly he left this world and our life together. As his spirit gradually departed the life of his physical body, I accompanied him on his final journey as far as I was allowed to go.

Twilight came and retreated as night encroached on our last hours together, each breath more labored than the last, heaving, and at last gasping. I tried bravely not to cry in his presence during the long vigil at his bedside as I sat there and watched him slowly die. My thoughts were random and escapist. My mind searched frantically for life even as I knew that soon he would be dead. I held his hand and talked to him. I rested my head on his arm, yearning for physical connection, somehow still believing that he would revive.

The sense of his spirit ebbing away was the dark backdrop of those last hours, his suffering and pain near their earthly end. Resignation and anticipation were the contradictions of my watch as I waited helplessly for the impending moment of death. The great empty space that would be my life without him at its center was beyond human imagination.

The truth is that it is absolutely impossible to comprehend or process the death of another person before the fact, however dire the circumstance. Hope persisted that the nightmare of his illness would yet end in earthly victory. Irrationally I expected him to rise up and say, "Come on, Jules, let's go home." I had no concept of what death would be like when it came, or how it would feel to experience the last breath of another beloved human being in a single moment of utter finality. In some inexplicable way, I expected to participate—not as a helpless bystander to his dying, but in the mystery of his actual death.

His entire body gave a great start around 12:30 a.m., as though to wake me from exhausted half-sleep, "sleeping through sheer grief" (Luke 22:45 JBP). With extraordinary physical strength he gripped my arm, his beautiful blue eyes feverish and suddenly wide open. What did he see to rouse his spirit from the coma of death to half-consciousness? Who was there? What did he hear? Why did it exclude me? The words from the hymn "To God Be the Glory" resonated: "our wonder, our transport, when Jesus we see."[1] Was this his experience of transport, his "going on toward perfection"? There was an intimation of eternity and of our spiritual immortality in that incomprehensible moment of silence so powerful it touched the very edge that separates mere mortals from life beyond death.

He held onto my arm as long as he could. I had so longed to see his beautiful blue eyes one more time. I did. When he closed them for a last time, his grip released. When the moment passed, I knew that his spirit had departed. I sat and watched as his beautiful body, devoid of spirit, lived on for two more hours, slowly, painfully, inevitably giving up the last of his physical being, breath by wordless breath. I could not believe that his life was almost over. It was only a moment ago that our life together was safe and ordered, every moment a joy.

He died at 2:40 a.m. It was the dark night of my soul. He left without me. He left without saying goodbye. "But now that he is dead, . . . can I bring him back again? I will go to him, but he will not return to me" (2 Samuel 12:23 NIV).

I was directed to an impersonal room where I waited, cold and in shock, for someone to complete the death certificate formalities. This ungrateful task was relegated to a rookie chaplain who was, at best, unpracticed in spiritual matters of dying and death. I heard myself saying words to encourage him in his fledgling pastoral care ministry. At my request, he walked me to the car.

Awkwardly he muttered a few words of superficial comfort. I brushed them aside, as though they were not intended for me. I was awash in disbelief that death had come, a death that was cruel, untimely, and unreasonable. I left that hateful place for a last time. I left without my husband. I was alone.

Driving toward home along the now familiar route, the car seemed to find its own direction. As I merged into freeway traffic with others speeding along at 3:15 a.m., my rage and anger found conscious expression. I cried aloud somewhere into the universe, "Doesn't the world know that my husband just died? Can't it stop for even ten seconds to mark the passing of a great man from this life?" Through my tears and exhaustion, I thought about how I was now among the cars on the freeway going somewhere, part of the anonymous, red-orange blur of pulsing motion I had observed from the window of my dying husband's hospital room . . .

> *Stop all the clocks, cut off the telephone,*
> *Prevent the dog from barking with a juicy bone,*
> *Silence the pianos and with muffled drum*
> *Bring out the coffin, let the mourners come.*
>
> *Let aeroplanes circle moaning overhead*
> *Scribbling on the sky the message He is Dead,*
> *Put crêpe bows round the white necks of the public doves,*
> *Let the traffic policemen wear black cotton gloves.*
>
> *He was my North, my South, my East and West,*
> *My working week and my Sunday rest,*
> *My noon, my midnight, my talk, my song;*
> *I thought that love would last forever: I was wrong.*
>
> *The stars are not wanted now: put out every one,*
> *Pack up the moon and dismantle the sun,*
> *Pour away the ocean and sweep up the woods;*
> *For nothing now can ever come to any good.*

"Funeral Blues," W. H. Auden (1907-1973)[2]

And so began my journey through grief. My story is not the same as your story. For each of us, grief is unique and personal. Yet we all share a common experience; we all know the painful reality of grief because we have lost someone we love. In this chapter, you will explore the nature of grief and the experience of grief.

What Is Grief?

"Now is your time of grief, but I will see you again and you will
rejoice, and no one will take away your joy."
John 16:22 NIV

The death of one you love is like the death of a part of yourself. Grief is the outpouring of emotion and pain that expresses how you feel because of what has happened in your life:

- Grief is shock at the suddenness with which life's plans have been changed.
- Grief is anger at the untimeliness of death.
- Grief is sadness.
- Grief is the pain of starting to speak to someone who is no longer there.
- Grief is going to bed without saying goodnight to one you love.
- Grief is an empty chair at the kitchen table.
- Grief is wandering around a too large house with painful memories.
- Grief is emptiness.
- Grief is loneliness.
- Grief is adjustment.
- Grief is reorganizing to go on with life.
- Grief is wishing that things were as they used to be and knowing that they never will be again.
- Grief is contemplation as you meditate on the finality of your own earthly life.

You grieve because of a loss you would never desire:

- You did not plan for your loved one to die.
- You could not control death—the when, where, how, or why.
- You are powerless to change what has happened.

Though universal in its fundamental attributes, grief is individual and personal. Just as everyone has a different story, so also everyone grieves differently. I do not grieve in the same way that you grieve, and you do not grieve in the same way that another grieves. The idea that it is possible to take charge of your grief belies the very nature of pain and heartache. No amount of resolve or discipline can determine the course of grief. In *Much Ado About Nothing*, William Shakespeare wrote, "Every one can master a grief but he that has it."[3] The head cannot lead; it must follow the heart.

A beloved person dies, departing your physical, earthly life together. Harold Kushner wrote, "When you have loved somebody, they have entered so intimately into the fabric of your soul that neither death nor time can ever take them out. They are always with you."[4] At first, you deny grief, mercifully shrouded by shock, fatigue, and numbness. In the emotionally arduous hours and days that follow, you function, still stunned by the bitter reality of death.

You experience rites and rituals with vague detachment from a surreal moment in time and space. When the last guest has left, you are alone. Grief assaults you like a tsunami. You may be engulfed by uncontrollable weeping—perhaps many times each day. When it descends upon you, grief is raw and gut wrenching—a state of soulless heartache with painful physical symptoms that mirror your emotional devastation.

I mourned openly and unashamedly. I wept spontaneously and without apology, freely and publicly, much to the obvious discomfort of many reluctant onlookers. I would not give in to accommodate the disapproval of transient mourners who participated in the brief funeral moment and quickly departed to avoid my profound grief. I defied convention. I would not succumb to discernable societal pressures all around me that suggested I should abandon my loss, even as I had been abandoned in death. I was certain that grief is an unpunishable offense. The thought of giving up my grief instead of moving toward it, encountering it, struggling with it, and going through it felt like giving in. I would not forego any part of the experience of grief necessary for the survival of my soul and spirit.

Grief has a life of its own. It is a restless shadow in the soul, for a while insistent and unavoidable. The dimensions of grief shift from day to day as you contend with the reality of life without your dearly beloved. How you incorporate grief into your life is the challenge of each new day.

Your life is shaped by how you deal with the unalterable circumstance of death. Grief never leaves you where it finds you. It leaves you disillusioned or more profound. It leaves you fearful or more confident in the faithfulness of God, depending on how intently you listen to what grief has to say.

In the Christian faith, grief is sometimes framed in self-denial. Many grieving Christians feel guilty for crying or being sad; their rationale is that a person of strong faith should feel happy to know that his or her loved one is in heaven. But grief is not a crisis of faith; it is a crisis of the heart. As a person of faith, you can believe beyond doubt that the one departed is with God, but you are human. You are in pain. You hurt. This does not mean that you are a bad Christian or that your faith is weak. Rather, grieving is really a show of faith. You trust God to hold you at your most vulnerable, when your life is in pieces, and your strength is gone. "The eternal God is your refuge, and underneath are the everlasting arms" (Deuteronomy 33:27 NIV).

God is with you as you grieve. God shares your tears and sadness; God feels your pain and sorrow. God is with you as you struggle in your brokenness. God promises that grief and pain will not last forever, that you will be restored and made whole again.

Death is nothing at all. It does not count. I have only slipped away into the next room. Nothing has happened. Everything remains exactly as it was. I am I, and you are you, and the old life that we lived so fondly together is untouched, unchanged. Whatever we were to each other, that we are still. Call me by the old familiar name. Speak of me in the easy way which you always used. Put no difference into your tone. Wear no forced air of solemnity or sorrow. Laugh as we always laughed at the little jokes that we enjoyed together. Play, smile, think of me, pray for me. Let my name be ever the household word that it always was. Let it be spoken without an effort, without the ghost of a shadow upon it. Life means all that it ever meant. It is the same as it ever was. There is absolute and unbroken continuity. What is this death but a negligible accident? Why should I be out of mind because I am out of sight? I am but waiting for you, for an interval, somewhere very near, just around the corner. All is well. Nothing is hurt; nothing is lost. One brief moment and all will be as it was before. How we shall laugh at the trouble of parting when we meet again!

"Canon of St. Paul's Cathedral,"Henry Scott Holland (1847–1918)[5]

In the remaining pages of this chapter, you will name the emotions and feelings of grief. Some may be uncharacteristic or unfamiliar to you. Framing what you experience in the context of grief will help you to understand better your emotional, physical, and spiritual reaction to loss. Be assured that you are not alone in your response to death and that grief does not last a lifetime.

Anger

"Peace I leave with you, My peace I give unto you; not as the world giveth, give I unto you. Let not your heart be troubled, neither let it be afraid."
John 14:27 KJV

When you grieve, anger is a common emotional reflex to your separation from the one you loved and lost to death. Yet anger is socially toxic. It is an emotion we all are expected to repress, ignore, and resolve, especially when we grieve. Seen as an inability to control negative emotions, anger is construed as a sign of weakness. Because society has little tolerance for the weak, you may feel pressure to conform to a life absent of anger. Yet when you deny or repress your anger, you may experience very real physical and emotional symptoms that mirror your grief and add to your pain of loss. You must acknowledge your anger, recognize it as a by-product of your grief, and work toward its positive resolution.

When you grieve, you are not prepared for the full frontal assault on your heart that occurs when anger shows up unannounced. It may surprise you with its force and power. Anger thrives and consumes vital energy if you provide a place in your heart for it to take root and grow. Eighteenth-century English poet Alexander Pope wrote, "To be angry, is to revenge the fault of others upon ourselves."[6] Instead of nurturing your anger, you must respond to it in appropriate ways.

> *On the day of Leighton's death, our internist called around 3:00 that afternoon. We considered him a friend, yet he had not attended us over the final, long weekend of Leighton's life. He did not visit, send word, or call. It was officially not "his" case, though Leighton was definitely "his" patient. I felt that he had failed us in his ambivalent leadership of the medical specialists entrusted with the care of an extraordinary life. At the "tipping point"[7] of life and death, he did not suggest, recommend, or in any way facilitate death with dignity. When*

he called that afternoon, he deftly avoided my specific questions. He made vague reference to infection, muttered his sympathy for my loss, and quickly disconnected.

The dam of my emotions broke. I wept, distraught at the insult of his clinical apathy and indifference, which compounded the mortal injury of my soul. He could not know my rage amid the unleashed torrent of grief.

An ominous bill from the surgeon's office arrived that same day in the mail. Fearing some dire consequence if I did not respond immediately, I called the surgeon's office the next day in a state of irrational anxiety. The doctor was unaware that his patient had died. My anger was death defying.

A first and important step in responding to your anger is to identify the reasons you are angry. You may be angry because:

- Your loved one died.
- You feel abandoned.
- You feel alone.
- You feel the pressure of new responsibilities.

The target of your anger may be:

- your loved one
- other family members
- doctors or medical personnel
- well-intentioned friends
- yourself
- God

It is hard work to sort through the emotions that engulf you after death, as you simultaneously reconcile yourself to loss. As you confront anger, you realize that it is not wrong to experience it as long as you understand its cause and manage it constructively. When anger occupies your thoughts, it easily instructs your guilt and regrets.

> *After Leighton's death, my spirit was tormented by guilt. I felt personally responsible that I could not save his life, guilty that we somehow failed each other at the end. I did not fail him, nor did he fail me. Failure can be assigned only if there is something that could have been done to change the outcome. There was not. One author states that when guilt haunts, it has a way of causing us to take some responsibility for death when we are, in fact, not responsible. Leighton's death was a rude encounter with my own humanness and my inability to alter the course of his mortality. I could not save him.*

For the survivor, grief encourages revisionist thinking in response to feelings of guilt and failure. Earthly life ends when death occurs, with no ensuing bad acts. The mind of the survivor filters selectively, minimizing shortcomings, idealizing the good, enabling sanctification of the one who has died. After Leighton's death, I remembered, memorialized, and cherished while struggling to make sense of that which could not be explained. I struggled to answer questions that would never be resolved and to reframe the bad to conform to the overwhelming good. Leighton once spoke these wise words in a sermon: "What God expects of us is trust, a loyalty that does not demand full understanding and a love that dares to trust God even when it cannot fully comprehend where our pain and misery and sorrow are leading us."[8]

Most survivors have some regret or guilt, whether imagined or real. We know the futility of that which "might have been"—our guilt and regret about the "could, would, and should" of grief. Your own regrets might be about words that should not have been said or words simply left unsaid:

- You might have talked more about the disease.
- You might have had a moment-of-truth conversation.
- You might have confessed your fear of death.
- Your loved one might have expressed more concern for your future.
- You might have said a real good-bye.
- You might have given or received forgiveness.
- You might have given or received a last kiss.
- You might have expressed your love more often.
- You might have spent more time together.
- You might not have had that last argument or disagreement.

Personal Reflections

I should have . . . I might have . . . If only I had . . .

_____

_____

_____

_____

As you begin to identify unresolved issues of guilt and regret, the space in your heart for the emotional legacy of the one who is gone will be cleansed and again made whole.

You can resolve your anger slowly as gradually you abandon it, giving your anger latitude and allowing it to abate over time. Or, there may be a time when you consciously let go of your anger, reaching a turning point in grief when you are unwilling to spend more of your precious mental resources on the nonproductive emotion of anger. In either case, you resolve your anger when you forgive. Naming your anger will help you to discern who or what it is you need to forgive.

In his book *When Bad Things Happen to Good People*, Harold Kushner observes that even the most devoted caregiver may experience that moment when fear and fatigue assume the guise of impatience and anger as exhaustion gives way to exasperation.[9] When you forgive yourself that you could not save your loved one from death, you commend your experience to the perspective of the past, enlarged to include your own humanness. As well, you forgive others their failures with you. When you forgive, you quiet trouble in your heart. You receive peace.

Personal Reflections

What are the personal issues of grief that make me angry?

Am I able to articulate clearly my guilt and regrets?

If not, why not?

What is my anger covering up?

What is the reason for my anger?

What purpose does my anger serve?

Will I experience any positive outcome from my anger?

Am I comfortable with my anger?

How is my anger affecting me and others?

How long do I want to invest in anger?

Is my anger a worthy emotional companion on my grief journey?

How long do I intend to sustain my anger rather than release it?

What am I doing to identify and resolve my anger?

What am I doing to release my anger?

Fear

"Do not fear, for I am with you, do not be afraid for I am your God; I will strengthen you, I will help you, I will uphold you with my victorious right hand."
Isaiah 41:10 NRSV

In his book *A Grief Observed,* C.S. Lewis wrote, "No one ever told me that grief felt so like fear."[10] In grief, likely you greet fear every day; for some it seems like every minute of every day. Fear is a normal part of the experience of grief.

Fear is "a feeling of agitation and anxiety; a feeling of disquiet or apprehension."[11] Grief magnifies your human capacity for fear. When someone close to you dies, what you most fear becomes reality. Feelings of agitation, anxiety, and apprehension reflect the fear of grief. Though fear is a common response to death, it need not permanently define life.

Eighteenth-century philosopher, orator, and politician Edmund Burke wrote, "No passion so effectually robs the mind of all its powers of acting and reasoning as fear."[12] Fear ambushes you when you are unprepared and least able to defend yourself. When you grieve, fear threatens to paralyze you. Fear has the power to make you feel incompetent and hopeless. Your confidence becomes self-doubt; your certainty becomes second-guessing.

For a while, strength and wisdom are reduced to weakness. Your world is shaken; you are wounded and broken. In the aftermath of your rude encounter with death, you may ask in quiet panic, "Who will be there for me now that my loved one has died?" You are vulnerable to the kaleidoscopic emotions engendered by fear:

- fear of illness and death
- fear of change
- fear of the unknown
- fear of the future

Other fears are more personal:

- fear of not having enough money
- fear of driving
- fear of living without your loved one
- fear of going to public places
- fear of loneliness
- fear that you will get hurt
- fear that you will die alone or lose someone else close to you

Writing in a journal can be a personal retreat while doing the arduous, daily, lonely work of grief. You are blessed when words pour forth, unexpected words that show you what you fear and help you to manage it.

Three weeks after Leighton died, it was time to renew my driver's license. At that time, renewal was like a vocabulary word in an obscure foreign language. I was much more familiar with expiration. There was a disconnect between the assumption that life would go on, symbolized by a renewed driver's license, and the bitter reality that life seemed over, that it had expired. I felt dead. The driver's license photo taken that day reflects the image of a vaguely familiar stranger wearing a shocked half-smile. My expression was beyond emptiness and personal anima. Five years would expire before the next renewal. I thought to myself that perhaps a new photo would expunge from my consciousness the reminder of that painful day.

Driving home, I felt rampant desperation, the active internalization of despair with the potential for dire physical consequences. The possibility of a heart attack or stroke seemed very real. I should not have been at the wheel of a car then, or at other times when I was a danger to myself and to others.

The need for an outlet to release some part, any part, of my emotional turmoil was imperative, perhaps caused by something physiological that occurs with the shock of a great loss. I wanted to understand the inestimable personal tragedy that had happened with such incalculable speed. I needed to figure it out. I knew I must assign some logic and reason to it that would make sense to my pragmatic mind and mitigate the incessant torment racking my body and spirit.

A vague impetus penetrated my consciousness. I felt directed to the bookstore for the clear purpose of buying a journal. I am an extreme left-brain person, organized and detailed. I am by nature perfectionistic, though not obsessive. Until that day, I had never kept a journal, not even a naïve adolescent diary.

The journal became my mental lifeline. It saved my sanity through months of shock and dark grief. After an elaborate and heartfelt inscription in the first beautiful black leather book—which I later would repeat in many subsequent volumes—I turned the page and began to write. I wrote and wrote. The floodgates of my mental anguish, guilt, and self-doubt burst open. My emotions at last found their voice—not necessarily my personal voice, but a voice from within that gave insight, perspective, and instruction, a kind of third-party self that gave comfort to my raw emotion and inconsolable pain. Today my journals are the recorded sequence of my arduous grief journey.

When you write about fear, you face it.

- You put it in perspective.
- You consign it to a safe, private place.
- You assess whether it is real.
- You recognize it as the temporary by-product of life in constant change.

When you do that which you fear,

- You turn it into courage.
- You disable its power.
- You defeat it.
- You become stronger.

Slowly you regain emotional equilibrium and self-confidence as fear dissipates.

God is our refuge and strength, a very present help in trouble. Therefore we will not fear, though the earth should change, though the mountains shake in the heart of the sea; though its waters roar and foam, though the mountains tremble with its tumult.
Psalm 46:1-3 NRSV

Personal Reflections
What is it I fear? What do I fear will happen?

What is the worst that will happen?

What will more likely happen?

What can I do to disable and conquer my fear?

Worry

"Therefore do not worry about tomorrow, for tomorrow will worry about itself. Each day has enough trouble of its own."
Matthew 6:34 NIV

In grief, your most faithful companion is worry. Concern, worry, and anxiety are often used interchangeably to express emotional distress. Concern easily escalates to worry as you assume greater responsibility for your life and the lives of others in your care.

The aftermath of death left me drained and exhausted. Each day I was compelled to stop at the end of my energies, whenever that occurred. I could not push myself mentally or physically beyond the limitations of grief. Grief demanded that I do routine business in slow motion, at mental half-speed. Because important decisions required wisdom and discernment, I could not be precipitant. So many issues seemed like failure to one so accustomed to success.

Fluctuations between complete gloom and glints of light were extreme and unsettling to one ordinarily so calm and level. My life teetered at the very edge of depression because of worry and fear of the unknown. Endless circular monologues of the mind, the interior conversations of grief, stretched my brain to the limits of cognitive tolerance. I worried about every small matter. Everything assumed a disproportionate importance. Where should I eat? What should I eat? Do I need new towels? Can I afford to keep our home?

The iron broke two days after the funeral. Buying a new one seemed a monumental task. It was a simple task, yet too large for my grief. It rained. The roof leaked. Fear was central to every large and small crisis. I worried and survived, waiting for life to be as it once was but would never be again.

Worry is a learned habit, an acquired state of mind and thought. Some people worry habitually; others are less predisposed to chronic worry. The emotional pain of grief intensifies worry. Your fears drive and inspire worry. When you grieve, worry is a natural reaction to questions you ask every day, such as "What should I do about . . . ?"

Anxiety expresses your fear. It is worry born of your grief-driven uncertainty and self-doubt. After death, anxiety may cause unaccustomed distress or panic. Anxiety is a visceral reaction to your fear of the unknown; it is your projection about that which may or may not happen. Anxiety is characterized by questions such as "What will happen if...?" and "What will I do if/when...?"

Agonizing is the most extreme form of worry. It is the non-productive response to your circular inner monologue, the endless conversation of the mind that asks, "What if...?" You agonize subconsciously when you anguish over:

- difficult decisions
- seemingly hopeless situations
- long-term possibilities
- unknown outcomes

You may ask yourself questions such as,

- How will I manage our children alone?
- Will I be able to fill the role of both mother and father?
- Will I be able to take care of the things my loved one managed for us?

As you grieve, remember that worry is a side effect of grief, not a permanent condition. You can defeat anxiety and conquer worry through persistent prayer with thanksgiving, quiet introspection, and personal meditation. Though you may be reluctant to share your concern, anxiety, and worry with another person, you may discover that entrusting your grief to the care of a trusted friend, a trained professional, a minister, or even those in your group will be a tentative though productive first step in overcoming worry. Gradually your life will become more manageable and less driven by fear and insecurity. You can be assured that God is larger than your worry.

Personal Reflections
What am I worried or anxious about now?

My Health
__The health of loved ones
__What will happen if I get sick?
__Who will be there to take care of me if I get sick?
__Where will I live if I get sick?

The Future
__What is my life about without my loved one?
__Will I ever be loved again?
__Will I ever love again?
__Will my children be there to love and support me as I age?

Financial Security
__Will I have enough money to live?
__Who can I trust with my money?
__Will I have a job and be able to work in the future?

Other: _____

Have I ever experienced extreme distress or panic? If so, when and why?

How do I respond to moments of grief-related anxiety?

Am I agonizing about anything now?

What are the ongoing questions that revolve in my mind?

How do I manage the incessant thoughts that worry my mind and spirit?

Suffering

But those who suffer he delivers in their suffering;
he speaks to them in their affliction.
Job 36:15 NIV

As a human being you are designed so that every measure of your capacity to enjoy higher values carries with it a corresponding capacity to suffer. The more sensitive you are, the more you suffer. If you did not love, you would not suffer.

Generally, suffering is associated with physical distress. When you grieve, you suffer the pain of loss. Physical suffering is often a manifestation of grief; grief and suffering are inextricably linked.

The perfunctory luncheon after the funeral for our small, fractured family was a blur. It meant nothing to me except the prolongation of my insistent urge to collapse. When the final "I thought they would never leave" guests departed our home, I moved about like an automaton, winding down, restoring order in slow motion as my spirit crumbled from within. Someone called to ask if I had gotten the house cleaned up: no word of comfort or condolence, only a sly, airy probe to see if I was back to "normal." What was normal or ever would be normal again in my life?

The power of Leighton's presence was palpable, his absence incomprehensible. Instinctively I listened at the back door, expecting at any moment to hear his car, his familiar footsteps, his physical being whole and well, greeting me in exuberant love. As my crumpled body found a sturdy corner, I slid down the wall, sat on my haunches, and sobbed in great heaving torrents as I capitulated, succumbing utterly to the suffering of grief.

Job is the historic paradigm for suffering. The patience of Job is a modern idiom. Patience derives from the Latin word *patior*, meaning "to suffer." Job patiently suffered affliction, yet he was not entirely passive. He wanted to know the reason; he wanted to know the why of his suffering. Job insisted that God meet him face to face and explain the injustice of it all. Why did God allow Job to suffer? There was never a clear answer. Yet because of his suffering, Job learned to humble himself and trust God.

In grief you, too, seek in vain for the "why" of death. In his book *Cries from the Cross*, Leighton wrote,

What most of us need in our adversity is not to find an explanation—but to find a victory; it is not to elaborate a theory—but to lay hold upon a power. Even if the best and most completely satisfying answer to our question "why?" was available, that would not alter the fact that the actual suffering would still have to be endured.

There is a deeper question than "why?"—namely, "how?" The ultimate question is not "Why has this happened to me?" but "How am I to face it?"...Not an explanation of what has happened, but the grace to...bear it.[13]

To *suffer* is "to bear, allow, let."[14] "Suffer little children to come unto me, and forbid them not: for of such is the kingdom of God" (Luke 18:16 KJV). That is, let the children come, allow them to draw near. As a beloved child, God calls you into God's presence to comfort you in both physical and spiritual suffering. Suffering invites you to place your hurt in larger hands, in God's hands. According to Swiss theologian Hans Küng, "God's love does not protect us *against* suffering. But it protects us *in* all suffering."[15] Suffering is part of life. It is part of what it means to be human.

Suffering is also "to endure or bear."[16] As you grieve, you may suffer attitudes and superficial platitudes offered as comfort, which hurt rather than help. The statement "God doesn't give you more than you can handle" is loosely based on 1 Corinthians 10:13: "No temptation has overtaken you except what is common to man. And God is faithful; he will not let you be tempted beyond what you can bear. But when you are tempted, he will also provide a way out so that you can endure it" (NIV). Temptation, however, is not the same as suffering in the context of grief. Similarly, the saying "It is God's will" explains away the death of your loved one as an act of God. This flawed premise denies your right to believe what you believe, to feel what you feel, to grieve as you need to grieve. Grief specialist Doug Manning states, "God does not gossip. . . . He does not talk to [others] about you."[17] No matter how convincing others may sound, they do not know the will of God.

At your most vulnerable, you may suffer familiar secular clichés as well, such as:

- I understand.
- I know how you feel.
- I know *exactly* how you feel.

The truth is no one knows how you feel except you.

You also may suffer pronouncements meant to console, presumptions that trivialize your grief:

- It's for the best.
- He is not suffering anymore.
- She is better off.
- He is at peace now.
- Everyone dies sooner or later. She just died sooner.

Naturally, you are angry, hurt, and upset when careless comments such as these add to your suffering.

You may hear other statements suggesting that your suffering is somehow wrong:

- You shouldn't feel that way.
- Keep a stiff upper lip.
- Be brave.
- Don't cry.
- You should have more faith.
- You ought to give away his or her clothes.
- You'll get over it in a couple of weeks.
- It's time that you pull yourself together.
- The children need you to be strong.
- What doesn't kill you makes you stronger.
- You've got to get on with your life.

The unstated directive in each of these statements is "It's time for your suffering to be over." Yet no one knows when that will be. Grief does not concede to those urging you to move on. Those who insist that you get on with your life do not appreciate that you may never "get over" your grief. Instinctively you resist every implied suggestion that you accelerate your return to life.

Friends and family who have not experienced your personal loss may be unaware of your need for nurture and understanding. You rationalize and forgive unintentional slights that hurt and confound you. Admonitions to be "done with grief" cause you painfully to recall the comfortless, infuriating funeral euphemisms, "He's in a better place" or "What a blessing." Words intended to comfort the broken heart overlay your pain and deny your loss. After all, who feels blessed when someone dies? And what is the blessing of death for those who remain in this world except the end of mortal pain and suffering for the one they loved?

Sometimes you may suffer what I call "at least..." assertions that discount your pain. There is little comfort in these empty words:

- At least he didn't suffer.
- At least her suffering is over now.
- At least it's not as bad as it could be. Things could always be worse.
- At least you don't have it as bad as.... There are worse things than death.

You suffer because you have loved and lost an important person in your life—perhaps the most important person. You may withdraw and become less communicative for a while, second-guessing your strength and faith. You suffer as long as there is pain. With unadorned spiritual forbearance, you name your pain in the vocabulary of grief. Only when rampant emotions run their course and gradually subside does your suffering moderate. In a sermon, Leighton once said this: "Suffering is a purifying experience. In losing a part of our lives or something we value, we are given . . . a clearer view of God. We come through suffering to see things—our lives, especially—not just as they appear, but as they really are."[18]

Suffering leaves an indelible mark on the soul, yet it may be the source of some of the greatest discoveries of life. Through suffering each of us understands better the things that really matter: the meaning of faith, hope, and love. In suffering you determine whether your faith is a superficial ornament of life or the essential foundation for all of life. In suffering you find your deepest experience of God.

If you believe that it is not God's intention that you suffer forever, how, then, do you help yourself through the suffering of grief? Let me suggest two practices that can help us.

First, be intentional about patience. There is perhaps no spiritual discipline more difficult than patience. We live in an age that insists on instant gratification and quick results—now. Patience is a gift of grief, a discipline taught by grief. It is listening—"Be still, and know that I am God" (Psalm 46:10 NRSV). Patience is waiting in faith for God's will to unfold in your life. Henri Nouwen said that one of the great questions of life has to do not with what happens to us, but with how we will live in and through whatever happens. Your assurance is that God is with you in your suffering and through your suffering. You trust God's promise. "But those who suffer he delivers in their suffering; he speaks to them in their affliction" (Job 36:15 NIV). You will not always suffer.

The second practice is prayer. You can identify with the humanness of Job: his tears, his doubts, his questions. God knows your feelings. God is never threatened by your emotions, especially those of grief. God longs for you to be open and honest so that you may receive comfort in this darkest hour of your life. God is trustworthy and understands your grief. You will find relief from your suffering when you ask God's help in prayer, when there are no words except, "Lord, help me" (Matthew 15:25 NRSV).

On a walk in the neighborhood one afternoon, I saw a little girl tangled in a bicycle with wobbly training wheels. I did not know her, but I heard her small, anxious voice cry out in distress, "Help me." I engaged her with words of kind assurance and comfort and helped her get unstuck. I put her small feet back on the pedals and pointed the way to her nearby home. Similarly, God is at work in your life as you grieve. God comforts you, untangles your life, and points the way toward spiritual safety and home. You suffer for a while, yet you are assured of God's care and steadfast love. God hears and answers your cry, "Lord, help me."

Personal Reflections
What words have I suffered that hurt instead of helped?

Have I forgiven the well-intentioned comforter who spoke them?

What have I learned from my suffering that will enable me to be a more sensitive comforter?

How is suffering affecting my capacity to be more compassionate toward others who grieve?

Prayer

I love the LORD, *because he has heard*
my voice and my supplications.
Because he inclined his ear to me,
therefore I will call on him as long as I live.
The snares of death encompassed me

...

I suffered distress and anguish.
Then I called on the name of the LORD:
"O LORD, *I pray, save my life!"*
Psalm 116:1-4 NRSV

One of the most confusing aspects of grief is prayer. When your emotions are in turmoil, it is difficult to focus the mind and spirit to pray. You may want to pray yet find no peaceful place within when your heart is consumed by anxiety and fear. After Leighton died, my mind was a chaotic jumble of thoughts. I could not believe that my random prayers made any sense at all to God.

Because of the experience of death, your expectations of prayer change. When you watch as a loved one dies, you may be spiritually debilitated by your own helplessness. In the urgent, quiet desperation that suggests impending grief, you may be unable to pray. Your fervent, whispered pleas for healing and restoration are answered, but not with yes. Through the heartache of death, you learn that the answer to prayer may be wait or no. If you pray for comfort and strength, the answer is always yes. All prayers are answered.

Personal Reflections
What did I pray for if I watched illness progress toward death?

What did I pray for if the death of my loved one was sudden or unexpected?

What was the answer to my prayer?

How did I react to the answer to my prayer—anger, disappointment, resentment, bewilderment?

Do I believe that my prayers for healing were unanswered?

Why do you pray? You pray because God asks you to share your inmost being with the One who created you. You pray because God cares for you, because God is interested in every detail of your life. You pray not to enlighten God, but to discern the mind of God. Prayer draws you closer to God; it deepens your relationship with God. Prayer reminds you that you are dependent on God and not on yourself. You pray because prayer alleviates spiritual weariness. God knows what you need before you pray, and God asks you to lift your broken heart in prayer that . . .

- is soul-searching and introspective
- allows listening and meditation
- is possible only within the silence of the heart
- seeks divine wisdom and insight

When your pain is all-consuming, you may resist the impulse to pray. God understands; God carries your broken heart. Your prayer receptors may seem broken. For a while, it may seem you cannot ask for or receive answers to prayer. When grief is new, rife with your churning human emotion, every thought may be a form of prayer, an unbroken stream-of-consciousness conversation with God rather than a formal ritual at a predetermined time of day. This is one way you pray through your grief.

You surrender your will to God's will when you pray. When you acknowledge in prayer that you are not in control of life or death, you experience a humbling moment in grief. Praying "Thy will be done" is seeking, finding, and doing the will of God, not living in passive helplessness at the mercy of an inflictive, punitive God. Leighton expressed it well in a sermon: "'Thy will be done' ought to be understood in the sense of perfect trust—a perfect trust in the perfect wisdom and perfect love of God himself. The will of God ought to be seen as that which is positive, affirmative, and active in our life. When we pray "Thy will be done," we are not praying for weary resignation or forced acceptance. We are not praying to be taken out of a situation but to be able to take it and conquer it, to defeat it and overcome it."[19]

A few months after Leighton died, I was at a gas station late one afternoon filling the car. I was still very tentative about life without him at my side. Even the most routine task challenged my very will to survive. A stranger approached me and introduced herself. She knew me, but I did not know her. My impulse was to withdraw in self-protection, yet her words touched the deepest place of my grief. She said that my name had been on her heart and that she was praying for me. It was a powerful moment. A complete stranger boldly dared to reach out and enfold me with spiritual care through prayer. As she turned away and left, I felt that I had been visited by an angel. Since that day, there have been other experiences in which God has used a stranger to minister to me.

Friends and family assure you that they are praying for you. If you feel unable to pray, you may allow the prayers of others to carry you for as long as you feel disconnected from God. It is not so much that you are unwilling to pray; when you grieve, the mind is in chaos, unable to offer more than the simplest expression of prayer. Even before you ask, you listen for the answer to your plea, "O LORD . . . save my life!" (Psalm 116:4 NRSV). The psalmist affirms that God answers:

> *Blessed be the LORD, for he has wondrously shown his steadfast love to me when I was beset as a city under siege. I had said in my alarm, "I am driven far from your sight." But you heard my supplications when I cried out to you for help.*
> Psalm 31:21-22 NRSV

Many who grieve find comfort in praying for their deceased loved one. For them it is an act of communion, the spiritual acknowledgment that he or she lives on, perfected in heaven. I found this to be true in my own experience.

As I meditated in church one Sunday morning a few months after Leighton died, I was surprised to realize that I was praying for Leighton and his well-being. Prior to his death, I never understood praying for the dead. In my prayerful reverie, there was spiritual resonance. And I received an answer: "He is alive; he is well." It was an answer that gave peace and comfort to my tortured soul.

Praying for one who has died is a religious tradition that is more Roman Catholic than Protestant. It is worth consideration as a possible resolution of grief, especially if you are struggling with lingering guilt and regret. Yet if you find yourself praying to the one who died as though you are praying to God, pause and remind yourself that God is God; your loved one is not a co-God.

Through prayer you grow spiritually; you are transformed and renewed. Praying not only for yourself but also for others helps you to abandon self-involvement and acknowledge spiritual needs beyond the horizon of your own grief. When you are intentional about praying for your family members—especially those affected by the loss of the person you grieve—for your friends and co-workers, for those on your church prayer list, and for those in need in the world, you direct your thoughts and spirit toward the power of God's presence at work in your life.

The psalmists were faithful in prayer. They offered their impassioned cries to God for others and about others, from the same place of personal loneliness and isolation that you experience in grief. Be blessed by the assurance of the psalms: "But God has surely listened and heard my voice in prayer" (Psalm 66:19 NIV). God listens; God is always there. God hears you when you pray and reaches into your heart with abiding comfort and strength.

Personal Reflections

Has someone unexpectedly reached out, acknowledged my pain and sorrow, and given the gift of prayer to me during my time of grief?

How has my prayer life changed because of the death of my loved one?

Do I pray "Thy will be done" from a different perspective? Is it harder to pray this now?

How have I been comforted by an answer to prayer?

What concerns and individuals beyond my own experience of grief am I praying for?

Who is in need of my prayers?

2
UNDERSTANDING GRIEF

2
UNDERSTANDING GRIEF

On a recent trip to New York, I landed at Newark Airport in New Jersey. From there, the most expeditious route into the city is through the Holland Tunnel under the Hudson River, which leads directly into lower Manhattan. To be honest, I was rather unsettled by the necessity of traveling at subterranean depths, for I had been in New York on September 11, 2001; I will never forget the fear and desperation of that horrible day. When we drove down the gradual incline into the tunnel, I knew that there was no turning back.

As I focused on the tunnel's rather nondescript, clinical-looking tiled walls, I thought of the infrastructure supporting this extraordinary feat of engineering. So much more than just those million bits of ceramic hold back the tremendous hydraulic power of water. I was reminded that the unseen framework of that remarkable man-made tunnel is an apt metaphor for God's unseen presence at work in our lives. I reflected that, as we grieve, God is the invisible foundation that holds and supports us. God is unshakeable and never changing.

In the middle of the tunnel, a light flashed on top of a slowing maintenance truck a short distance ahead. My mind automatically raced through several worst-case scenarios. Traffic slowed and then gradually stopped. The driver of the truck hopped out and quickly changed places with a colleague at the mid-way monitoring station. Apparently, it was lunchtime. The entire exchange took perhaps five seconds. We gradually moved forward again and ascended as light slowly bathed the end of the tunnel in the golden warmth of hope.

Light had been there all along—over, above, and outside the tunnel—unseen for the moments of my travel from a suburb into a city, moments spent in a place of relative darkness submerged under a body of water. So it is on your journey through grief. You descend for a while with no turning back as you enter a dark place. There are obstacles and stops along the way, yet you trust God, the infrastructure, to keep you safe. As you emerge from the tunnel of grief, darkness is at last overcome by the light of renewed life. It is the light of God's eternal love that guides your way through the dark passage that is grief, "for we walk by faith, not by sight" (2 Corinthians 5:7 NRSV).

In this chapter, as you explore the story of David and the death of his son, the stages of grief will be illuminated for you.

The Stages of Grief

[David's] servants asked him, "Why are you acting this way? While the child was alive, you fasted and wept, but now that the child is dead, you get up and eat!" He answered, "While the child was still alive, I fasted and wept. I thought 'Who knows? The LORD may be gracious to me and let the child live.' But now that he is dead, why should I fast? Can I bring him back again? I will go to him, but he will not return to me."
2 Samuel 12:21-23 NIV

In her book *On Death and Dying*, Dr. Elisabeth Kübler-Ross identifies five stages of emotional and psychological response that most people experience when faced with a life-threatening illness or life-changing event: denial and isolation, anger, bargaining, depression, and acceptance.[1] It is important to note that Kübler-Ross originally studied these stages *only in people suffering from terminal illness.* Only later were they applied to any form of catastrophic personal loss.

The Kübler-Ross stages best describe the clinical structure of dying, death, and grief in the abstract. Understanding the stages may help in the diagnosis of grief. But when we grieve, we do not live in a constant state of clinical self-awareness. Seldom are we consciously aware that we are in a particular stage of our emotional response to death.

As we experience grief, we reference where we are and how we feel rather than the clinical structure of grief suggested by stages. When we grieve, few of us have the mental focus to self-diagnose, to remark to ourselves, "I am in the stage of denial and isolation." Instead, when we are in this stage, we feel shock—indeed, we are often immobilized by shock.

> *The day of Leighton's death marked the onset of shock. By no other protection of nature could I have continued to function as calls were made, the news spread, and the dreaded funeral rituals unfolded. Despite my complete emotional and physical exhaustion, I heard myself comforting others. My capable, stalwart exterior belied the devastated interior version of myself. My outside and inside did not match. I soldiered on. I existed despite the sudden, unexpected event of death. It was a death witnessed on a collision course. For me, it was death in the first person.*

At each moment we do not name a stage of grief; rather, we struggle through it with only the will to survive. For this reason, in this book and in the group sessions, we will explore the spiritual and emotional issues of grief without persistent reference to stages.

To best illustrate the stages of grief, our biblical narrative describes the incipient grief of David, an acclaimed warrior, a musician, and the poet of many psalms:

> After Nathan had gone home, the Lord struck the child that Uriah's wife had borne to David, and he became ill. David pleaded with God for the child. He fasted and went into his house and spent the nights lying on the ground. The elders of his household stood beside him to get him up from the ground, but he refused, and he would not eat any food with them.
>
> On the seventh day the child died. David's servants were afraid to tell him that the child was dead, for they thought, "While the child was still living, we spoke to David but he would not listen to us. How can we tell him the child is dead? He may do something desperate."
>
> David noticed that his servants were whispering among themselves and he realized the child was dead. "Is the child dead?" he asked.
>
> "Yes," they replied, "he is dead."
>
> Then David got up from the ground. After he had washed, put on lotions and changed his clothes, he went into the house of the LORD and worshiped.

Then he went to his own house, and at his request they served him food, and
he ate.

His servants asked him, "Why are you acting this way? While the child
was alive, you fasted and wept, but now that the child is dead, you get up and
eat!"

He answered, "While the child was still alive, I fasted and wept. I
thought, 'Who knows? The LORD may be gracious to me and let the child live.'
But now that he is dead, why should I fast? Can I bring him back again? I will
go to him, but he will not return to me." (2 Samuel 12:15-23 NIV)

A man of strength, David lived in conflict with himself, torn between ambi-
tion and lust, and his desire to serve God. This sounds like our contemporary
dilemma doesn't it? The actions of David at the death of his beloved son model
our struggle through the stages of grief. Like David, we act and react. We per-
sonalize structure as we move toward the resolution of our grief.

Your reaction to the experience of illness and death is an integral part of your
grief journey. If your loved one endures the debilitation of illness, you suffer
alongside in *denial and isolation*. Perhaps frustrated by your own helplessness—
you are unable to save him or her, not so much *from* death but *for* life—*denial* at
first protects you from that which is incomprehensible: all the force of your human
will cannot alter the event of death. As reality slowly replaces *denial*, you begin
to forgive yourself your powerlessness over death. Slowly you release your lingering self-recrimination. Once you are able to abandon your imagined failure,
you are better able to comprehend the reason for your seemingly irrational behavior whenever you are in *denial* over death.

"After Nathan had gone home, the LORD struck the child that Uriah's wife
had borne to David, and he became ill" (2 Samuel 12:15 NIV). It is important for
you to ask yourself what you believe. Do you believe that God strikes us down?
Do you believe that God causes us to become ill? Do you believe that God determines whether we live or die? Or do you trust in God's plan for life set in motion
by mysteries that God alone comprehends? When we have no answers to the
mysteries of life and death, we often react in *anger*.

"David pleaded with God for the child. He fasted and went into his house
and spent the nights lying on the ground" (2 Samuel 12:16 NIV). David did what
we do, especially when calamity strikes our lives. He pled with God; he was *bargaining* for the life of his child. When faced with the reality of illness and death,
did you plead with God to spare the life of your loved one or change your
circumstances in some way? As a survivor, do you find yourself bargaining with
God? As part of your bargaining, have you performed sacrificial acts as an offering to God?

"The elders of his household stood beside him to get him up from the ground, but he refused, and he would not eat any food with them" (2 Samuel 12:17 NIV). Focused only on the vigil at the bedside of your loved one, or awash in grief after your loved one died, did you ignore the urging of others to eat and sleep? Have you denied yourself human care and sustenance as self-punishment for your imagined failures?

"On the seventh day the child died. David's servants were afraid to tell him that the child was dead, for they thought, 'While the child was still living, we spoke to David, but he would not listen to us. How can we tell him the child is dead? He may do something desperate'" (2 Samuel 12:18 NIV). The fear and dread expressed by the servants may sound like a doctor, nurse, hospice worker, or family member you encountered who was reluctant to be the herald of bad news. Were others protecting you from death? Were they afraid to tell you the truth? Were they fearful of your reaction? Were you in denial about imminent death?

"David noticed that his servants were whispering among themselves and he realized the child was dead. 'Is the child dead?' he asked. 'Yes,' they replied, 'he is dead'" (2 Samuel 12:19 NIV). David was not spared the harsh reality of death. No one relied on the euphemisms of death—"He passed away," "He's gone," "He's not with us anymore" to communicate the truth to David. The words used to express the fact of death affect you: "He is dead." "She is dead." Often these words signal the onset of grief and *depression.*

"Then David got up from the ground. After he had washed, put on lotions and changed his clothes, he went into the house of the LORD and worshiped. Then he went to his own house, and at his request they served him food, and he ate" (2 Samuel 12:20 NIV). After David was told that the child was dead, he took action. He got up from the ground. Likely, it was cold, hard, and dirty; perhaps it was like the uncomfortable sofa or hospital recliner that was your resting place for days or weeks. After the death of your loved one, did the first shower or bath seem ritualistic or normal and cleansing? Did a steady stream of running water allow you to escape from the reality of death for even ten minutes? David then anointed himself with lotion and put on some fresh clothes. He took time to take care of himself. He took the first step to prepare for the rest of his life without his beloved child.

Finally, David demonstrated his spiritual strength. He went into the house of the Lord and worshiped. We practice our faith at funeral and memorial services, yet often we are incapable of true worship at the time because the unfamiliar emotions of grief overwhelm us. Because we are in shock, worship often seems almost counterintuitive.

David then went home and asked for food. He was hungry and wanted to eat. He realized that his fast had not changed the course of the child's illness or death. Did others implore you to eat after the death of your loved one? Did you resist, indifferent to their insistence?

"His servants asked him 'Why are you acting this way? While the child was alive, you fasted and wept, but now that the child is dead, you get up and eat!'" (2 Samuel 12:21 NIV). Uncharacteristic behavior is part of grief. It is, in fact, an inalienable right of grief. We are irrational. We scarcely feel sane. We are not ourselves. We may weep uncontrollably and reject the comfort of others. We may refuse to take care of ourselves. The narrative suggests that David returned to his routine easily and quickly; most likely, the biblical timeline of events is abridged. As his grief subsided, David gradually resumed a semblance of normalcy. He neared *acceptance* of the death of his son. He went on in life as the second king of the united kingdom of Israel.

"He answered, 'While the child was still alive, I fasted and wept.' I thought, 'Who knows? The LORD may be gracious to me and let the child live'" (2 Samuel 12:22 NIV). David had a rationale for what he did. His strategy was fasting and weeping as his bargain with God. He was powerless, yet he tried to change the course of the child's illness through self-denial. He dared to imagine that the Lord might heal his child and hoped in God's grace.

"But now that he is dead, why should I fast? Can I bring him back again? I will go to him, but he will not return to me" (2 Samuel 12:23 NIV). David knew with certainty that the child would not return to him. He was equally certain that he would be with the child again. Likewise, our faith affirms that we will be reunited with those we love who have died: "I will go to him, but he will not return to me." Like David, we trust in the compassionate care of God. In life, as in life beyond death, our faith triumphs over every stage of grief.

The Journey of Grief

Even though I walk through the valley of the shadow
of death, I will fear no evil, for you are with me.
Psalm 23:4 NIV

In this familiar, beloved passage, the image is that of the shepherd guiding his sheep through many terrains and perils to reach hillside grazing and safety. The psalmist writes, "Even though *I* walk through the valley of the shadow of death." He uses the first person, "*I*." We know that the one who dies goes *into* that symbolic valley toward the finality of death, yet we as survivors actually go *through* the valley of the shadow of death. We encounter this place of powerful metaphor as we descend the depths to meet our wounded soul at its most vulnerable, scaling the exigencies of loss and adjustment. Slowly we make our way to the other side as at last we journey through grief, our personal valley of the shadow of death.

The experience of grief is often referred to as a journey. A journey is usually longer and more difficult than a short trip. Grief is personal. It is a first-person journey.

One lonely Saturday afternoon a few months after Leighton died, I sat in a movie theater and was struck by advertising for a well-known brand of luggage. As travel images flashed on the screen, the message unfolded that a journey is not a trip or a vacation. Rather, a journey is both a process and a discovery. As a process of self-discovery, a journey brings us face to face with ourselves. On a journey, we not only see the world; we also understand better how we fit into the world. Although I did not rush out and buy the advertised luggage, the final teaser was powerful. The question posed was whether the person creates the journey or the journey creates the person. In less than sixty seconds, the message was clear: "The journey is life itself. Where will life take you?"

When we grieve we ask, "When does the journey begin?" The journey starts when grief begins, whether on the actual date of death or at some time during a period of illness or physical decline.

My journey began when Leighton got sick, suddenly and unexpectedly. From the outset, life went steadily downhill, steeply declining into the abyss of disbelief and desperation. April 25 was our seventeenth wedding anniversary, our last together. It was a bleak, forlorn day marked by a return trip to the pharmacy for more home medical supplies. I was helpless and exhausted. My frustration raged. Our whole life was spinning out of control (as though somehow we ever had any control at all). In complete emotional surrender, I bowed my head on the steering wheel of the car and wept bitterly. My tears mourned the day. We always celebrated our special day with cards, an elegant dinner, and romance. A part of me died that day as I confronted the reality of his illness. The relentless downward spiral encouraged my raw fear of the inevitable outcome. Everything seemed so hopeless. And it was only the beginning.

When he died, our earthly life together abruptly came to an end. He left the valley of the shadow of death as I ventured alone, an emotional stranger, into the unknown dark chasm of grief.

None of us knows the destination of our grief journey. Have you ever set out on a trip without some idea of where you were going, the best way to get there, or when you would arrive? The unknown path of your journey through the valley of the shadow of death is what makes your grief so arduous.

- Your unexpected setbacks are detours.
- You have unplanned side trips when you become unexpectedly ill or disabled.
- Your emotional ups and downs keep you on the uneven pavement of a bumpy road.
- Your interactions with those who do not understand your grief isolate you on the rough shoulders of a narrow, less-traveled highway.

The murky road looms ahead with no end in sight. Its large, garish billboards shout, "What is your destination?" "When will you be there?" "How will you know when you are there?"

Not long after Leighton died, I went to Shreveport to visit a beloved aunt who was infirm. I was visually assaulted by the message of a billboard as it shouted at me in twenty-foot-high letters, "God is in control." This stark visual admonition both comforted and convicted me. In that graphic moment, I was confronted again with the most sobering reality of death and grief: We are not in control. We are not in charge of anyone or anything except our own attitudes and emotions. No matter how much I loved Leighton and longed to rescue him from his inevitable demise, I could not control his life or death. God is God. God is in control. I am not God.

Almost five years later another billboard loudly proclaimed, "He is there and He is not silent." This public affirmation of the power and presence of God in our lives seemed very personal to me. When we are attuned to the billboards along the way on our journey through the valley of the shadow of death, we discern our direction and our destination.

Consider with me the analogy of a car and driver. From the moment of death, grief is in the driver's seat of your life. It is your silent, steady companion in charge of the journey until its end. Like a cab or bus ride, you entrust your safety and your very life to a driver personally unknown to you.

Perhaps you rode in a limousine to the funeral or graveside service for your loved one. This means of transportation is often more a necessity than a luxury at the time. Perhaps, like me, you were grateful that you did not have to drive yourself.

A limousine ride can be pleasurable, but if you are the only passenger and no else is along for the ride, there is nothing and no one for you to hold on to. Every turn feels like a boat careening around a sharp corner. As the lone passenger, you are tossed about in random motion like the spin of a carnival ride or the thump and bump of a clothes dryer. This is the journey of grief—solitary and chaotic. You have no control over the route. An unfamiliar force is in control of your life until you arrive at your destination.

Reluctantly, you become acquainted as grief drives on. You engage in conversation; you want to know more about this driver in charge of your life. Somewhere along the way, you switch cars and downsize to a luxury sedan that is more stable and comfortable than the limousine. As you progress still further along the journey through grief, you pull over and want to drive yourself again.

You switch to your accustomed vehicle, which is smaller than a limousine or luxury sedan. You prefer your own car because it is more proportionate to your life, scaled down to its more accustomed size. You order grief into the backseat, knowing that its unavoidable presence will be with you yet for a while, until someone else needs a capable driver. Car and driver is indeed one apt metaphor for life on the journey through grief.

With uncertainty, we ask how we are to traverse the valley of the shadow of death. "Even though I *walk*..." (Psalm 23:4 NIV). We are not asked to jog, run, or race. We walk. Our journey through grief—through the valley of the shadow of death—is slow, laborious footwork. We put one foot in front of the other. Sometimes we walk only one half-step at a time. But our direction is always forward. We do not walk backward. We may look over our shoulder and cast a backward glance, but we walk forward through the valley of the shadow of death.

Along the way, we lose our balance. We may miss a step. Our footing slips and we fall down. We recover our toehold, we dust ourselves off, and we again inch forward, gaining ground after each setback. We may attempt great bounding strides to deal with grief as quickly and expeditiously as possible. But grief will not be hurried or bypassed. We learn that there is no easy detour around it. The slow, steady pace of a rhythmic walk will ultimately see us through to the other side. On the road, we acquire the courage, strength, and self-nurture necessary for life after loss.

Those who have walked the road of grief before us have left behind a well-worn path. Their testimony of stamina and fortitude strengthens us for our journey through grief. When we follow in the steps of another who has grieved, we discover that death has redemptive value because loss and survival inspire us to greater compassion for the suffering of others. We then become trailblazers for those whose grief is newer than ours, to whom we offer the humanity and wisdom of our life because it has been tried and tested by grief.

Our journey through grief is nuanced by contrasts of light and dark, which create shadow. We recognize this in our lives as the long shadow cast by death. "Even though I walk through the valley of the *shadow* of death..." (Psalm 23:4 NIV). Think with me about the idea that inherent within shadow is the suggestion of light. Without light there can be no shadow. In art, chiaroscuro is the distribution of light and shade. It is the use of deep variations and subtle gradations for dramatic effect, as in the paintings of Rembrandt. We make our way through the valley of the shadow of death because light is hidden within the shadow. We persevere through grief because at the end of the journey there is the promise of radiance.

You may be new to the emotional time travel of grief. You may be reliving every footstep of the journey, counting the days and weeks since the death of your loved one. Or you may have been on the road for months, perhaps even years, weary from the endless road. Grief is not time that has done its work, as many would say; rather, we do the work of grief to the point of mental, spiritual, and emotional exhaustion.

> *Time Is*
> *Too Slow for those who Wait,*
> *Too Swift for those who Fear,*
> *Too Long for those who Grieve,*
> *Too Short for those who Rejoice;*
> *But for those who Love,*
> *Time is not.*
> Henry van Dyke (1852–1933)[2]

Gradually we learn that our perspective is the compass that points the way. Where we are now enlightens the past and suggests the future. Time reframes what happened into how we live forward; time allows us to reflect with more than a rearview mirror. Novelist Kathleen Norris writes, "I have learned to trust the processes that take time, to value change that is not sudden or ill-considered but grows out of the ground of experience. Such change is properly defined as conversion, a word that at its root connotes not a change of essence but of perspective."[3]

The Journey of Grief

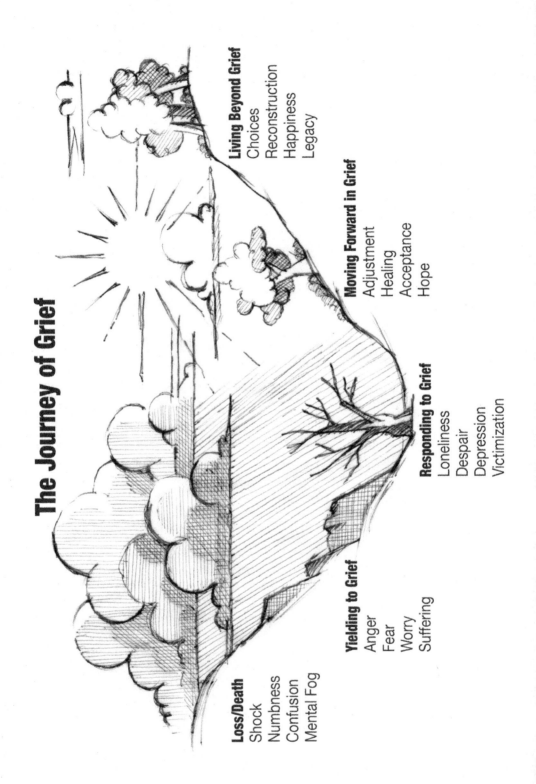

Loss/Death
Shock
Numbness
Confusion
Mental Fog

Yielding to Grief
Anger
Fear
Worry
Suffering

Responding to Grief
Loneliness
Despair
Depression
Victimization

Moving Forward in Grief
Adjustment
Healing
Acceptance
Hope

Living Beyond Grief
Choices
Reconstruction
Happiness
Legacy

This diagram of the journey of grief is a road map of the valley of the shadow of death that suggests where we are along the way. The words used to describe the topography of the journey through the valley of the shadow of death are personal, expansive, and accurately characterize our grief. We might define *topography* best as "the lay of the land." It is how the ground looks, both where you have been and on the road ahead.

Each person has a different topography, a unique landscape of grief, because each person starts at a different point. Think about the topography of your own grief journey:

Personal Reflections
Did I jump off a cliff into the valley of the shadow of death because of the sudden illness or death of my loved one?

Was I overwhelmed by a landslide of illness that went nowhere but down?

Was I a caretaker or caregiver for several years before death? Is my map one that reflects persistent erosion?

Was the death of my loved one like the slow, steady, white-hot flow of lava down a mountainside?

The geography of your grief journey includes places and settings that will never be the same again without the one who is gone. If you move from a family home, your physical place of daily life changes. You no longer inhabit the space in which a life together was created and nurtured. You may be unable to enjoy a favorite restaurant or a shared travel destination. You may avoid an accustomed church pew or a place that evokes powerful emotion or memory. Along the way, your head and heart signal your direction. When you pay attention to the signs, you see where to go and what to avoid. Your head may say, "go" but your heart may say, "broken—stop—don't go." As the geography of grief changes topography from deep valley to expansive plain, it may be less painful, perhaps even pleasurable for you to revisit places you once abandoned because of your grief.

As you grieve, you create a personal map that charts where you are going in life without your loved one. Your map may be like that of Christopher Columbus and his contemporaries. Early explorers expected to fall off the edge of the earth because they were unable to imagine life beyond the visible horizon on distant shores or in undiscovered places. Yet the allure of what might lie beyond inspired them to risk everything. They embarked into the future with faith that God would be there to lead them, to light their way, and to direct their path. This is your quest on the journey through grief as well. God charts your map through the valley of the shadow of death. God faithfully leads you beside still waters. God restores your soul.

God's divine destination for you at the end of the journey is peace. Peace does not overwhelm you all at once and for all time. You are not suddenly there. Your peace comes in small, elusive moments when fleeting glints of emotional sunshine warm your heart and then fade. Your moments of peace recur with greater frequency until your life is more about contentment than pain and more about peace than grief.

- You are at peace because you have forgiven yourself your human insufficiency to death.
- You are at peace because you no longer strain against that which you cannot change.
- You are at peace because you have traversed the valley of the shadow of death and survived the journey through grief.

You know that you are near the end of the journey when you claim for yourself the gift of peace.

> *My Lord God, I have no idea where I am going. I do not see the road ahead of me. I cannot know for certain where it will end. Nor do I really know myself, and the fact that I think I am following your will does not mean that I am actually doing so. But I believe that the desire to please you does in fact please you. And I hope I have that desire in all that I am doing. I hope that I will never do anything apart from that desire. And I know that if I do this you will lead me by the right road, though I may know nothing about it. Therefore I will trust you always though I may seem to be lost and in the shadow of death. I will not fear, for you are ever with me, And you will never leave me to face my perils alone.*
> Thomas Merton (1915-1968)[4]

Personal Reflections

Where have I been?

Where am I now?

What are my obstacles along the way?

If I have been on the journey for a while, am I moving forward?

Where are my oases for quiet and rest?

Where is my place of "still waters"—a glassy lake, a seaside retreat, a reflecting pool, a burbling fountain?

What are the signposts along my journey?

What are the billboard messages I have received?

What is my destination?

3
YIELDING TO GRIEF

3
YIELDING TO GRIEF

The story of my journey through grief would be incomplete if it did not include my father's illness and death. My beloved father first showed signs of decline around 1995. The generic diagnosis was Alzheimer's and Parkinson's disease. Although his deterioration did not conform to the textbook description of either condition, the outcome was the same. His slow but steady downward progression over ten years—punctuated by medical crises that led to greater incapacity and disability—ended in death after two final years spent in excellent institutional care.

Through the stuttering synapses of Alzheimer's disease, my debilitated father, once so smart, wise, and strong, asked me with childlike incomprehension, "But how did I catch this cancer?" He did not have cancer. He never had cancer. Yet his question resonated with truth as I quested simultaneously with bare-knuckle determination to understand how in fact Leighton had "caught this cancer."

From the moment I was born, my father and I shared a rare, impervious bond of filial love. We cherished our relationship. We were friends. We were confidants, business associates, and trustworthy allies within a complex, often fractured family dynamic.

I see little girls with their fathers and think wistfully of our Saturday rambles together. I was loquacious and amusing; he was at once delighted and enchanted. Our relationship was unshakeable, occasionally tested yet tried and true. I knew him better than anyone else knew him; I loved him more than anyone else loved him.

As he gradually succumbed to the illness of his old age, our roles at last reversed. I became the parent, he the child. Throughout his decline, he graciously allowed me to provide leadership and advocacy. I likened my father's demise to that of watching an ice sculpture melt. The once strongly defined figure was disappearing drop by drop, with no hope of salvaging the sculpture from the watery puddle or somehow reconstructing it, as though to make it whole again and renew life from without and within. It hurt my heart to see him going away. I struggled. I cried out loud, "How long, O Lord? How long?" It was a sacred privilege to be there for him, holding his hand until his last dying breath, honoring his life even in death. Ours was a sweet parting, private and personal. He was eighty-six years old when he died in 2005. I loved him. He loved me.

Leighton died out of sequence; he died before my father. I have lost the two men I loved most in the world. The words of the old hymn overwhelmed my spirit, "God helps the stranger in distress, the widow and the fatherless."[1] In Psalm 146:8-9 God promises, "The LORD lifts up those who are bowed down....[he] sustains the fatherless and the widow" (NIV). It was unimaginable that I became both within eight short months.

Grief is both loneliness and solitude. In this chapter, you will consider the difference between the two. When you grieve, it is difficult to find rest for your soul, yet this is a promise of God's love and care for you. Finally, you will explore the meaning and expressions of comfort in your life as you yield for a while to grief.

Changing Through Grief

Blessed is the man who perseveres under trial, because when he has stood the test, he will receive the crown of life that God has promised to those who love him....

> *... Every good and perfect gift is from above, coming down from the Father of the heavenly lights, who does not change like shifting shadows.*
> James 1:12, 17 NIV

When your loved one dies, everything changes. Yet when you grieve, you resist every change thrust upon you. From the lessons of life, you learn that change is the constant of time. But you are assured that God is the one constant that does not change, "the Father of the heavenly lights, who does not change like shifting shadows" (James 1:17 NIV). As you yield to grief, you understand that it is your "shifting shadow."

The experience of death teaches you that the ordinary is precious. Through the heartache and sorrow of grief, you realize that your days with your loved one were a treasure. Author Mitch Albom has observed, "We often fantasize about a perfect day, but when it comes to those we miss, we desperately want one more familiar meal, even one more argument."[2] When you grieve, you yearn for the ordinary and you desperately want the familiar. In his poem "To a Skylark," Shelley reflects, "We look before and after, And pine for what is not."[3] You want life to be the same as it once was. You want your life back. The hard reality of grief is that everything has changed. From the first bad news of illness, accident, or sudden death, grief becomes an active participant in your life. It may feel to you like an ominous cloud of eternal darkness. But grief is more a shifting shadow, one that obscures all of life for a while then whispers away as it passes. Grief shifts as you experience certain inevitabilities that affirm the reality of the death of your loved one. These signal events might include, but certainly are not limited to, the following:

You attend a probate hearing.

Our attorney prepared me for the probate hearing six months after Leighton's death. He could not anticipate the shock to my fragile psyche when an original copy of Leighton's will, signed in blue ink, was presented by a court clerk for me to witness. I saw Leighton's robust signature, which made him still alive for me in that short, irrational moment of utter disbelief. With the insensitivity of a practiced bureaucrat, the clerk asked me to attest, affirm, and verify the cold legal document that irrevocably proclaimed, "He is dead." My heart broke all over again at yet another bitter confrontation with the abrupt reality of death.

You settle the estate of your loved one.

It was painful to undo the details of Leighton's life, to deconstruct the business of seventeen years of marriage and thereby announce to the world, "He is dead." My ungrateful task was to cancel, to re-order the daily, and undo the earthly infrastructure of a life built together to last forever, "until death do us part."

We thought we would be together "for the rest of our lives." We expected our life as one to go on and on. For him this was reality, for me not. So I wonder anew each day what "the rest of my life" is to be.

You attend to the disposition of things.

Because Leighton had been gone from home for over two months during his stay in the hospital, his clothes already seemed dispossessed of their owner. Leighton had a small wardrobe of beautiful clothes that he enjoyed and wore elegantly. He related to me with flattered amusement an encounter with a small boy at the church who, dazzled by a gentleman wearing a suit and tie, looked up at him and remarked in awe, "You are a very pretty man." This tidbit became part of our private vocabulary for complimenting each other.

We shared the belief that the acquisition of things necessitates a corresponding stewardship of use. It was not difficult to dispose of his clothing within a few weeks after his death. As I sorted and made the necessary decisions, it felt like something I could take charge of and control after being so disempowered by the forces of sickness and death.

I smelled every item, hoping for a whiff of his fragrance or the scent of his body. It was all clean and pristine, as was his life. I was searching for any remaining vestige of his physical life, a hair or a flake, willing him to come back and be present to these things, his things. But his clothes lacked any endowment of his spirit. He cared nothing for the things of this world as possessions. He was not his things.

In your "shifting shadow" moments, you are forced by the business of life to face your loss. As reality dawns, shock slips away. You may feel that your grief is naked and exposed. As you are forced to change, you learn that grief is both adapting to change and growing into change.

Grief modulates as gradually its power to direct your every mood and moment subsides. As you change, you begin to reframe your grief to include the steady presence of your loved one, safely ensconced forever in your heart. Despite the inevitability of change, you are sustained by your memories, which are the most precious and sacred part of the past. You will never, ever forget.

Death is what happened to change your life forever. There is no benefit to reliving the past; the outcome will always be the same. No revisionism is possible, yet scraps of memories still float up and around you, reminding and assuring you that the past was real.

Your earthly life together with your loved one happened. Nothing can void or erase what you had in whatever lifetime you shared together. The reason is that love remains. Your love will always be. This will never change, despite all the other changes taking place around and within you.

Inherent in grief is its power to change you. Grief can affect you negatively or positively. Grief can make you:

Stronger	or	Weaker	or	Embittered
More Faithful	or	Disillusioned	or	Spiritually Isolated
More Capable	or	Disabled	or	Dysfunctional
Independent	or	Dependent	or	Helpless
Wiser	or	Stubborn	or	Willful
Deliberate	or	Impulsive	or	Rash

Personal Reflections

How is my grief changing?

How is grief changing me?

Loneliness

And after you have suffered for a little while, the God of all grace, who has called you to his eternal glory in Christ, will himself restore, support, strengthen, and establish you.
1 Peter 5:10-11 NRSV

Loneliness is the overarching experience of grief. When you find yourself suddenly without your loved one, loneliness is the pervasive condition of your heart that spans the duration of your grief. For a while, loneliness is the steady, ice-cold companion of grief.

> *The life Leighton and I shared together was good, filled with joy and happiness. We shared a relationship so close, so intensely personal, that there was fusion of the "I" into a formidable, perhaps impenetrable, "we." His death left me forcibly, physically un-fused and de-fused. I was bereft and in complete despair.*
>
> *Everything changed when he died. My loneliness drove me to a solitary place deep within that left my spirit tear-stained and aching. I missed him so much I could hardly breathe. I missed him every day and a thousand times on Sundays.*

You long to express your grief. You want to talk about your emotional isolation and loneliness. Part of the loneliness of grief is the urgent desire to keep your loved one alive in your heart and mind. You feel the need to talk and invoke his or her name and continuing spiritual presence. You want to hear others speak with passion about the life and enduring legacy of your loved one. But who is listening, really listening? Who understands your pain and bewilderment?

> *The erroneous perception by others of my towering strength precluded the intimacy and emotional vulnerability required to share my profound grief. There was no one of depth, compassion, or personal experience that I trusted to listen thoughtfully, who would allow me to talk and pour out my heart without judgment or easy, formulaic advice. I was not ready for professional counseling or therapy. I did not believe*

that I could be truly heard or understood by another human being. Several months later someone whose husband had died several years before, when she was the same age as I was when Leighton died, listened to the profound grief of my heart and understood my pain. She was a new friend, a soul friend.

Henri Nouwen recognized the importance of sharing your story while grieving. In his book *The Inner Voice of Love: A Journey Through Anguish to Freedom*, he wrote,

> The years that lie behind you, with all their struggles and pains, will in time be remembered only as the way that led to your new life. But as long as the new life is not fully yours, your memories will continue to cause you pain. When you keep reliving painful events of the past, you can feel victimized by them....
>
> There are two ways of telling your story. One is to tell it compulsively and urgently, to keep returning to it because you see your present suffering as a result of your past experiences. But there is another way. You can tell your story from the place where it no longer dominates you. You can speak about it with a certain distance and see it as the way to your present freedom.[4]

In addition to magnifying your desire to talk about your loved one, the awkwardness of loneliness will magnify your fear and emotional insecurity for a while. One of the most challenging aspects of grief is eating alone. The empty chair at the kitchen table is always a frustrating encounter with your inescapable loneliness. Meals together with family were daily communion, a celebration of life and each other. You shared conversation, ideas, plans, and dreams.

The fact is that you must eat to nourish your body. This is the way God created you. Yet in grief, you may become indifferent to your own care and self-nurture. The neglect of proper diet and nutrition is a common manifestation of loneliness. You are forced to reconfigure this part of your life, adopting new habits that honor God's gifts of physical health and well-being.

Months after Leighton died, I was still trying to figure out eating at home and eating out. The nutrition part of my life made me feel unsettled and always at odd ends. The frustrating quest for "survival" that food literally and figuratively represents was an ongoing, daunting challenge. It was a miracle that I did not end up weighing 1,000 pounds. I sought comfort in comfort food, but there was no comfort there. I found that nothing really satisfied the emptiness that was both emotional and physical. I tried and did a little better. That was gratifying, at least for a moment. I made the effort to eat real food that was nutritious and satisfying, rather than processed food. I did what I could to improve that part of my life, meager as my efforts were.

Your loneliness stands in sharp contrast to life going on all around you. In grief, your impulse may be to both isolate and insulate yourself because you are alone. Until death changed your life, you were among the carefree, happy people laughing and perhaps holding hands in easy emotional communion with your loved one.

Everywhere I looked after Leighton died, I saw couples all around me. Some held hands and seemed very married, as Leighton and I were. Some seemed disconnected, living parallel yet apart. I wondered why some couples lived together into old age, and I wondered why I was now alone. I wondered why some seemed merely to tolerate each other yet stayed together in marriage, and I wondered why I was without my beloved.

You help to relieve your isolation and loneliness when you reach out to others. You might consider these possibilities for reaching out to connect with others:

- Find someone with whom you may speak freely about your loved one, ideally someone who has experienced a similar loss. Expressing your emotions will make you feel better.
- Share with others who understand that loneliness is part of grief. In addition to your *Beyond the Broken Heart* group, you may wish to become part of an ongoing spiritual, social, or community support group.
- Find an objective listener who will offer professional perspective on your personal issues of grief.
- In the words of Dag Hammarskjöld, "Pray that your loneliness may spur you into finding something to live for, great enough to die for."[5]

In March 2004, Leighton went to visit a close personal friend who had terminal lung cancer. He loved his friend, Dick, and was sad that he would soon die. Leighton cherished this final visit, touched by Dick's faith and unfailing good spirit.

Three weeks after Leighton died, I read the obituary notice for Dick. It was unimaginable to me that Leighton had become ill and died before his friend. Urged by my own grief to greater compassion for the heartache of another, I wrote a note to Dick's wife, whom I had met only once. Several days later, she called. I did not know her, yet she became my grief friend. We felt safe and comfortable talking with each other. We understood each other's pain and sorrow. We listened and helped each other. I found a friend, a new friend who was on the same journey through grief. We still talk occasionally, less often than at first. We grieve, we remember, we live.

Personal Reflections

Have I actively sought out and found a confidential grief friend? If not, how might I do this?

In what ways am I comforted by community within the shared experience of grief?

What dispels my loneliness?

In my loneliness, am I mindful of the need for "something to live for, great enough to die for"?

Solitude

In quietness and confidence shall be your strength.
Isaiah 30:15 NKJV

Solitude is aloneness without loneliness. It is the quiet within peace as you befriend your aloneness. Solitude is the peace that "surpasses all understanding" (Philippians 4:7 NRSV). Solitude is the incubator of the listening heart, the stillness within self-understanding that renews your strength.

The quiet heart waits in yearning patience
To find the mind of God.
"The Quiet Heart," John Ness Beck (1930-1987)[6]

In grief, you will learn that solitude and loneliness are not the same. When you intentionally pursue time alone for yourself, solitude can be both beneficial and emotionally productive. According to Henri Nouwen, "[Solitude] means daring to stand in God's presence . . . alone in God's company."[7] Alone means completeness within your own being—*all + one*. The late psychologist, writer, and television host Eda LeShan wrote, "When we cannot bear to be alone, it means we do not properly value the only companion we will have from birth to death—ourselves."[8]

Solitude is being alone without being lonely. Solitude is comfort within the confines of your own being. Protestant theologian Paul Tillich wrote, "Our language . . . has created the word 'loneliness' to express the pain of being alone. And it has created the word 'solitude' to express the glory of being alone. . . . Loneliness can be conquered only by those who can bear solitude."[9]

Sleep is nature's way of ensuring solitude. Your body and mind are restored through the power of silence. Statesman William Penn wrote to his children, "True silence is the rest of the mind, and is to the spirit what sleep is to the body, nourishment and refreshment."[10] God is with you in silence and in solitude.

Where is solitude amid the white noise of the world in which you live? You may find solitude in both aloneness and the presence of others. Solitude is a state, a destination for your spirit that is intermittent and unpredictable. Like Thoreau discovered at Walden Pond, solitude may be an intentional choice of place or time that nourishes your soul and welcomes you into communion with yourself.

Solitude inspires the courage of your own self-awareness as you adjust to the fluctuations of grief. In solitude, your inner voice speaks. This is the voice of both your conscious and subconscious minds; it always requires solitude to be heard and understood. Your inner voice is the steady participant in the internal, circular conversation of your mind. During my own journey through grief, stray thoughts constantly swirled through my mind as memories banged around my head and heart. When I consciously released them, or better yet discarded them, space was made for others to burble up in their place. If you listen, your inner voice clearly articulates to you the deep, unfathomed emotions well beyond your conscious thoughts. At that place of oneness within yourself, from the depth of your subconscious your inmost feelings illuminate your grief.

Once again, the bravery of day succumbed to the dark solitude of night. As I lay in our bed, his side was empty. I called into the room for what must have been the thousandth time, "Where are you, my love? Where are you?" There was silence. My being was still. And at last the answer came. "I am here in your heart, precious girl." Then there was peace.

Well beyond the expanse of your own inner voice, in solitude your eternal spirit is able to focus on the voice of God speaking to you through the Holy Spirit. We must listen intently to hear what God says to us in grief. Scottish theologian William Barclay wrote,

> God is not silent, and again and again, when the strain of life is too much for us, and the effort of his way is beyond our human resources, if we listen we will hear him speak, and we will go on with his strength surging through our frame. Our trouble is not that God does not speak, but that we do not listen.[11]

Solitude is not withdrawal from life in monastic silence or antisocial behavior. Solitude is not a way of life; rather, it is a way of finding life. In his poem "The Church Porch," seventeenth century poet George Herbert urged, "By all means find some time to be alone. Salute thyself and see what thy soul wears."[12] Solitude is an innate need, especially as you grieve. After the death of your loved one, you require the space and quiet afforded by solitude to do the work of grief. As Henri Nouwen noted, "Solitude, where we absent ourselves from the myriad voices that tell us otherwise, helps us hear again that voice of love."[13]

According to Roman Emperor Marcus Aurelius, "Nowhere can man find a quieter or more untroubled retreat than in his own soul."[14] Solitude reconciles your experience of death to life. Your soul-searching questions of grief are resolved through the enrichment of solitude with answers found only in the quiet of the heart. The soul at one with solitude invites the power of the Holy Spirit to comfort and restore. "In quietness and in trust shall be your strength" (Isaiah 30:15 NRSV).

The following reflections often find expression as prayers of the grieving heart. Listen in solitude for God's direction. Attune your heart in quietness to God's guidance. Wait in trust for God's answers. Accept in peace that some answers will never be revealed this side of heaven.

Personal Reflections
Why did my loved one die?

Why am I still alive?

What am I alive for?

Do my children still need parenting?

Am I here to influence and support my grandchildren?

Am I here to serve others in the world?

What is the purpose of my life?

What is the meaning of my life?

How do I find my way in life?

Rest for Your Soul

"Come to me, all you that are weary and are carrying heavy burdens, and I will give you rest. Take my yoke upon you, and learn from me; for I am gentle and humble in heart, and you will find rest for your souls.
For my yoke is easy, and my burden is light."
Matthew 11:28-30 NSRV

Grief is work. It is a full-time job, a 24/7 occupation. It is physically exhausting to grieve. The things of this world necessitate physical chores that layer your grief with fatigue. Duties and responsibilities once shared with another are perhaps now yours alone. Or, if you have lost a parent, additional duties and tasks may now be your responsibility. Grief demands your energy. Grief appropriates your personal reserves and depletes your emotional resources. When grief is at the forefront of your every thought and action, it is almost unimaginable to think about letting it go. Yet your own self-nurture mandates that you lay aside your grief from time to time to rest.

Grief is a tireless companion on your journey through the valley of the shadow of death. If you have ever traveled to an activity destination that was more exhausting than relaxing, or been on a trip that felt more like work than pleasure, the moment comes when you must rest. You cannot drive one more mile or sleep in one more uncomfortable bed. You stop at a nearby motel or hurry home to reach the comfort of your familiar environment. In grief, as on all arduous journeys, your body and spirit demand that you rest.

You move forward in grief, yet setbacks are inevitable. You must rest before you try again. When they occur, setbacks feel like a complete undoing of your hard-won progress. It may seem as if you are taking one step forward but two steps backward. This is when you rest. Your gains in grief are slow and incremental. Imperceptibly, grief becomes two steps forward and one step backward. You grieve forward and then you rest.

> *I saw a beautiful white bird in the sky one day and stopped the car to watch it soar upward. It floated up and then stopped to glide—soaring, then gliding. I longed for that fluid upward motion in my life, flying up then gliding to rest.*

One way that you rest from grief is by releasing your emotions through tears. Science reports that crying releases endorphins, brain chemicals that function as pain relievers and mood elevators. Because tears are cathartic, you usually feel better after you have had a good cry. There may be times when you have cried so much that you feel physically spent—at the end of your resources. This is the moment that you rest.

- Tears are the expression of the deep feelings that reside beneath the surface of your fragile exterior that words cannot express. When words fail, tears are the messenger.
- Tears are cleansing. They wash away some of the emotions that trouble you in grief.
- Tears are honest. Denying your tears prevents you from working through pain.
- Tears are healing. Crying releases tension and physical distress.

You can rest in the assurance of Revelation 21:4, "[God] will wipe every tear from their eyes. Death will be no more; mourning and crying and pain will be no more" (NRSV).

Jesus said, "Come to me, all you that are weary and are carrying heavy burdens, and I will give you rest" (Matthew 11:28 NRSV). When you grieve, you work at grief, sometimes to the point that the burden of it all seems unbearably heavy. *The Message* states it this way, "Are you tired? Worn out? Come to me. Get away with me and you'll recover your life. I'll show you how to take a real rest. Walk with me and work with me—watch how I do it. Learn the unforced rhythms of grace." To recover your life, you must get away with God. God's promise to you is rest. God invites you to learn "the unforced rhythms of grace," wherein you will find rest for your soul. "Take my yoke upon you," Jesus said, "and learn from me; for I am gentle and lowly in heart, and you will find rest for your souls" (Matthew 11:29 NRSV).

I sat at the Arboretum on a lovely spring day, writing in my journal as I reflected on life and love and loss. The sun on my neck felt at once cool, tranquil, and serene. It was peaceful in that place; it was the first conscious moment of rest for my soul. I mused that this sparkling instance of oneness with the world, of inner calm and refreshment, was perhaps the first perfect pearl on a new string of small jewels that would encircle my heart, adorn my spirit, and bring new light to my soul.

When attuned to your grief, you likely find that you receive your best insights when you listen to the still and quiet within your heart that is rest. So . . .

- Find rest for your body.
- Find rest for your mind.
- Find rest for your heart.
- Find rest for your soul.
- Find rest from your grief.

You may put down your load for a while, but like any faithful companion, grief waits while you rest. When you return, it will be there waiting for you, though not as insistent as before. Rest. Find rest for your soul.

Personal Reflections
What setbacks have I experienced?

What is the best description of my burden in grief?

How do I rest physically from grief?

What do I do to rest spiritually from grief?

Comfort

Praise be to the God and Father of our Lord Jesus Christ, the Father of compassion and the God of all comfort, who comforts us in all our troubles, so that we can comfort those in any trouble with the comfort we ourselves have received from God.
2 Corinthians 1:3-4 NIV

The word *comfort* is from the Latin phrase *com fortis*, meaning "with strength." To be comforted is to be made strong. As you grieve, your comfort and strength come from the power and presence of the Holy Spirit. Jesus promised, "And I will ask the Father, and he will give you another Comforter who will never leave you" (John 14:16 AMP).

The day after Leighton died was the most tragic moment of my father's illness for me. I had been to the funeral home to view the body of my husband. My anger was raging at the commercial indignities of death. Anguished, I went to see my father, hoping against hope that he would recognize me and could be again—even for an instant—my Daddy. I needed him to comfort me.

I knelt beside his wheelchair and wept uncontrollably. I begged him in my tear-soaked voice to understand what had happened, that my beloved Leighton had died. He smiled benignly. He was unable to react or respond to my great sorrow.

My father was always my great comforter. At any moment, he was ready to wipe away my tears, hold me close, and comfort my hurting heart. When I was a little girl he would take out his large white handkerchief, dab my cheeks, and gently murmur, "Don't cry, Julie baby, don't cry." As he kissed away my hurt, he comforted me as only a father can.

On that horrible day after Leighton died, I wanted my father to dry my tears. I needed him to assure me that he loved me and that everything would be all right, whatever "everything" was. It was a defining moment in his illness and another conscious letting go of a beloved person in my life. It was a moment of grief upon another more profound grief.

A comforter is one who consoles. The One who can "comfort those in any trouble" (2 Corinthians 1:4 NIV) is our Comforter. I was blessed with a father as my comforter. Your comforter may be a mother or a grandmother. Your comforter need not be a parent, though. It is anyone who can comfort you in trouble. We rest in the assurance that God is always our Great Comforter through the power of the Holy Spirit who never leaves us.

Personal Reflections
How have I been comforted by God?

Who else has been a comforter to me?

Who penetrates my sadness with unspoken understanding?

Who gives me emotional strength?

Who inspires me with hope?

Who is the safe person who responds to my grief with kind, thoughtful intentions?

To grieve toward growth, you must forgive your would-be comforters, those who try to console you with empty words or gestures. You expect others to understand what you are feeling, but it is not possible. You alone know the depth of your personal experience of grief. The truth is that no one can comfort you to your expectations; nor can you grieve to the expectations of another. Grief is not a job with a performance standard.

Think for a moment about the nuances of comfort that sometimes qualify your grief. Perhaps you are experiencing the discomfort of mental and bodily distress as you struggle to adjust, adapt, and accept the death of your loved one. Childcare experts offer diverse opinions about whether to let an infant cry when it wakes at night because of some real or imagined discomfort or to allow the child time to soothe and self-comfort back to sleep. Certainly, you would hasten to comfort a helpless child, but how do you comfort yourself through the discomfort of grief? As you explore and develop your instinct for self-comfort, you understand better that which truly comforts you in moments "beside the still waters." Much as a child finds solace in a worn blanket or favorite toy, your discomfort is transformed as you learn to comfort yourself better.

When you are overwhelmed by grief, you may be truly un-comfort-able, that is, unable to receive comfort from others or from God. For a while, it is not possible for you to be comforted by anyone or anything. Your deepest desire is not comfort as much as it is the return of life as it was. How, then, do you open your heart to receive comfort? One way is through praising God in prayer. In the Kaddish, a Jewish prayer said in memory of the dead, there is nothing about death. The power of its comfort reaches beyond death to extol the greatness of God in a memorial prayer in praise of God. The Psalms also include a wealth of prayers poured out in praise of God, such as,

> *I waited patiently for the* LORD;
> *he inclined to me and heard my cry.*
> *He drew me up from the desolate*
> *pit, out of the miry bog, and set*
> *my feet upon a rock, making*
> *my steps secure.*
> *He put a new song in my mouth,*
> *a song of praise to our God.*
> *Many will see and fear,*
> *and put their trust in the* LORD.
> Psalm 40:1-3 NRSV

In a sermon on "Grief and Death" Leighton said, "Our lives are in the hands of a loving, caring, merciful God. God cares about us. God cares about us in our moments of grief; God cares about us in our moments of death. I can commend to you a God who loves you, cares about you, who will hold you in his arms if you will let Him."[15] As he spoke, he poured the power and passion of his faith into the word *cares*. Neither he nor I could know at that time that his words of grace and comfort were meant for me.

God's comfort affirms the reality of the unseen as the very definition of faith: "Now faith is being sure of what we hope for and certain of what we do not see"

(Hebrews 11:1 NIV). Certainly, you cannot prove it, but likely you have had evidence of the abiding spiritual presence of your loved one in some way that affirms the reality of the unseen. Perhaps something occurred that you know without question was an unmistakable sign or signal that you alone would understand. Its power and force affirmed to you the real, eternal presence of your loved one.

> *I sat in church one day celebrating in community the rite of infant baptism. When asked to name their tiny daughter, the proud parents said "Leighton." In the moment that the name was spoken, he was there with me. His presence was so powerful it took my breath away. He was everywhere—beside me and within me. I knew then as I know now that he lives in eternity. I believe in the reality of the unseen.*

God explains more of the mystery of trust in the reality of the unseen in 1 Corinthians 13:12: "Now we see but a poor reflection as in a mirror; then we shall see face to face. Now I know in part; then I shall know fully, even as I am fully known" (NIV). For now, the reality of the unseen is a mystery. It is God's mystery of life and death. God's comfort is in the reality of eternal life, which is the very promise of faith.

> *As Leighton lay dying, the only world event that captured his attention was the death of President Ronald Reagan. We sat together watching the solemn funeral, silently denying that this ritual would affect us both imminently. I was profoundly moved by the anthem, which was the familiar "Jerusalem" hymn tune by C.H.H. Parry set to words by Horatius Bonar. Less than one month later, the National Cathedral arrangement was procured for use at Leighton's funeral service. The words would become my personal mantra of comfort through grief:*
>
> *O love of God, how strong and true!*
> *Eternal and yet ever new,*
> *Uncomprehended and unbought,*
> *Beyond all knowledge and all thought.*
>
> *O love of God, how deep and great!*
> *Far deeper than man's deepest hate;*

Self-fed, self-kindled, like the light,
Changeless, eternal, infinite.

O heavenly love, how precious still,
In days of weariness and ill!
In nights of pain and helplessness,
To heal, to comfort, and to bless.

O wide embracing, wondrous love,
We read thee in the sky above,
We read thee in the earth below,
In seas that swell and streams that flow.

We read thee best in Him who came,
To bear for us the cross of shame;
Sent by the Father from on high,
Our life to live, our death to die.
....
We read thy power to bless and save,
Even in the darkness of the grave;
Still more in resurrection-light,
We read the fullness of thy might.

O love of God, our shield and stay,
Through all the perils of our way;
Eternal love, in thee we rest,
For ever safe, for ever blest.

"The Love of God," Horatius Bonar (1808-1889)[16]

4
RESPONDING TO GRIEF

4
RESPONDING TO GRIEF

A few months after Leighton died, I ventured to New York, my city of retreat and respite. There was no relaxation on the trip, only a desperate sense of being completely alone in the world. It was an act of brute courage to leave home in my state of unremitting pain and despair. Returning three days later to a house that echoed its very emptiness broke my heart all over again.

While in New York, I bought a party dress—with no party to attend and no one to take me there. Though we were not at all partygoers, somewhere in my grieving mind I fancied an occasion that would justify the dress and make me feel that I was again part of life as it had been. Life as it should be. A life now as dead as my husband's body, as dead as the human impulse of my own spirit.

The dress was made of beautiful dark blue, corded satin, a dress unlike any I had ever seen. Another generation would have called it a frock. It was designed to be worn slightly off the shoulder and had a stylishly full skirt that swished when it moved. It fit my indifferent body to perfection. When the dress arrived several days later, I opened the package but never even took the dress out of the box. I wondered who had ordered it. In the days between its purchase and delivery, I realized my folly and forgave myself this retail absurdity. I grieved the abandonment of this imagined part of my life, a life that had once been but would never be again. I pitied myself for the loss of hope. Hope for a future, any future. I returned the dress without apology or explanation. This irrational purchase defined the disconnect between life as it had been and life as it now was.

On the same trip, I bought some party shoes. I guess they were supposed to go with the dress. I put them away and discovered them months later in a drawer. In a drawer? I had only a vague memory of this purchase. What had I been thinking? Nothing. At the time, I must have been just a little crazy, out of my mind with grief.

As you begin to understand how you are responding to death and grief, you will have the opportunity in this chapter to examine your attitude about what has happened to change your life. You may recognize yourself and your personal struggles in the consideration of courage. Finally, you will see that there is a difference between choosing to live the rest of your life as a victim or as a survivor.

Making an Effort

Let us therefore make every effort to do what leads to peace and mutual edification.
Romans 14:19 NIV

Life takes an effort, whatever the circumstance or quest. Grief demands that you make an effort in order to survive. The scripture says, "Let us therefore *make every effort* to do what leads to peace and mutual edification." As you make an effort, you respond to grief by growing in your capacity for peace and mutual edification. What is mutual edification? It is the encouragement and comfort you experience when you share your grief within the safe community of a group on the same journey through grief as you are.

The assumption of grief is that you are supposed to "do" something to help yourself. Effort and trying are the assumptions of doing. At first, all you want to do is succumb to heartbreak. This is the right time in grief to do nothing. Your body dictates your limitations; it insists that you rest. You must do nothing for a while to recover physically from the initial phase of grief that is emotional trauma and shock.

At the pool of Bethesda in Jerusalem, an angel of the Lord came down from time to time to stir up the waters. The first one into the pool after each such disturbance would be cured of whatever disease he had. A man sitting beside the pool had been an invalid for thirty-eight years. When asked, "Do you want to be made well?" he replied, "I have no one to put me into the pool when the water is stirred up; and while I am making my way, someone else steps down ahead of me" (John 5:6-7 NRSV). He wanted to be healed, but physically he was helpless. He was unable to manage his infirm body into the pool by himself. His effort was not enough to get ahead of those who were more mobile and able-bodied.

Similarly, perhaps you are challenged by the death of your loved one to try in new, unaccustomed ways to "get into the pool."

- You try to find where you fit in life without your loved one.
- You try to adjust to single life if your spouse is deceased.
- You "try on" new ways to live, perhaps alone for the first time in life.
- You "try out" new people or routines.
- You try to adapt to the expectations of others.
- You try new experiences.
- You try to go on with life.

Trying may feel like failure or like unexpected success. In fact, trying may feel like a full-time occupation. Yet every small victory is progress in grief. There are no real failures when you try.

I resolved to attend church again after the five-month hiatus of sickness and death. I wanted once again to be a congregant at the church where Leighton and I met and fell in love. In mid-September, a new worship service was being started in the chapel where we married. I summoned my courage and spiritual resolve and made the physical effort to attend.

I dressed, drove, and parked. I observed myself doing these things from somewhere outside of my mind and body. From that vantage point, I saw an unfamiliar stranger going through the motions, walking, entering, and sitting. I saw others, and they saw me. They saw my groomed exterior, but they could not see my shattered heart or know its cavernous emptiness. When others spoke to me, their conversation was hollow in my ears, their words an echo of meaningless sound that made my head ache. My spirit seemed dead. I was present yet absent, going through the motions intended as worship.

There was no song on my lips and little praise in my heart. I brought only my tear-stained face and a mortally wounded soul to worship the very God whom I perceived had cruelly punished me with the death of my beloved husband. In my heart, I knew that this was not true, for this is not the nature of God. But that is how it felt. It was very real at the time. Over months of meditation, my experience conformed to theology. Worship was no longer about me but about the rightful praise of a loving, caring God, the God of everlasting arms. "By the tender mercy of our God, the dawn from on high will break upon us, to give light to those who sit in darkness and in the shadow of death, to guide our feet into the way of peace" (Luke 1:78-79 NSRV).

Your place as a vital member of society and as a contributor to humanity is now perhaps unfamiliar because you are alone. Trying is using your talents and interests to give to others. Trying is using your unique, God-given gifts and graces to serve others. Trying is using your personal expertise to go beyond yourself in grief.

> **If making an effort seems consistently overwhelming to you, it may be time for you to seek the help of a confidential, non-judgmental counselor, therapist, or minister who will listen thoughtfully to understand your grief. The guidance of a qualified professional may be critical for your understanding of specific, individual issues that can hinder your progress in responding to grief.**

There is no guarantee that effort alone will ease the void once filled by the love and energy of the deceased. It will always matter to you that you have loved and lost; it will never not matter. Because it matters less to the world, you must make the effort to accommodate life as it surrounds you. Trying means staying connected to the world, a world that is not waiting on you or for you. Trying is an obligation of grief.

You honor your loved one when you reenter the world and endow others with your spirit. Your reentry may unfold gradually, in small increments, or there may be a moment of personal resolve to try. When you acknowledge that your life is here and now, and at this place, you may be more willing to make the effort.

Making an effort and trying are "doing" actions that may affirmatively transform you in life. Your charge in grief is to try, to "make every effort to do what leads to peace and mutual edification" (Romans 14:19 NIV). Make the effort. Try. Respond to your experience of grief.

Personal Reflections
What is difficult about making an effort when I am grieving?

What motivates me to find a new, unaccustomed place for myself in life?

What help have I enlisted—or might I enlist—to overcome the inertia of grief?

What are some of the failures I have experienced while making an effort?

What are some of the small victories I have experienced while making an effort?

Attitude

Do not conform any longer to the pattern of this world, but be transformed by the renewing of your mind. Then you will be able to test and approve what God's will is—his good, pleasing and perfect will.
Romans 12:2 NIV

The experience of most people in grief is that life seems out of control on many levels. You exist for a while in a dense fog. Unfamiliar mental chaos, distraction, and confusion impair your best judgment. You lack information and understanding, which may be the cause of much of your fear, anxiety, and helplessness. You learn through the experience of grief that you are not in control of the circumstances of either life or death.

The fact is that the only thing you can truly control in grief is your attitude. Everything precious, including your dignity, can be taken from you, but the one thing that cannot be taken away is your power to choose the attitude you will take toward events that have happened. Through the right attitude, unchangeable suffering is changed into a heroic and victorious achievement.

Austrian neurologist and psychiatrist Victor Frankl, a Holocaust survivor, believed that we find meaning in life within our attitude toward suffering. In his bestselling book *Man's Search for Meaning,* he relates this experience:

> Once, an elderly general practitioner consulted me because of his severe depression. He could not overcome the loss of his wife who had died two years before and whom he had loved above all else.... [I] confronted him with the question, "What would have happened, Doctor, if you had died first, and your wife would have had to survive you?" "Oh," he said, "For her this would have been terrible; how she would have suffered!" Whereupon I replied, "You see, Doctor, such suffering has been spared her, and it was you who have spared her this suffering—to be sure, at the price that now you have to survive and mourn her." He said no word but shook my hand and calmly left my office. In some way, suffering ceases to be suffering at the moment it finds a meaning, such as the meaning of a sacrifice.
>
> Of course, this was no therapy in the proper sense since, first, his despair was no disease; and second, I could not change his fate; I could not revive his wife. But in that moment I did succeed in changing his *attitude* toward his unalterable fate inasmuch as from that time on he could at least see a meaning in his suffering.[1]

When you grieve, you must simply feel what you feel for a while. With only the will to breathe, often you struggle merely to survive. As shock fades, you first name anger, fear, worry, and loneliness with unaccustomed emotional honesty. When you engage and respond fully to grief, your work then becomes reconciling your attitude about what happened to change your life with the reality of life as it is becoming.

For months, my heart seemed locked up from the inside. I was reluctant to let down the barriers to allow something larger than my own small world to touch me and move my grief-hardened heart. Was there nothing in my heart except this passionless emptiness? In my darkest moments of grief, life seemed to be more about dying than living. At those times there seemed to be nothing left inside me. Had Leighton's death so permanently affected my capacity for joy that I did not even want it? I confess that the idea of having any joy ever again in life without him seemed strange.

I worked at this part of my grief; I tried, I persevered. Yet I still felt cold within, loveless and a stranger to joy. I could not muster joy. There was no one and no thing that could give me joy or bring me joy. It was an experience from within that God alone could revive in my soul. Yet I wanted to live—in fullness of life and fullness of joy. I entertained the idea of joy again in life and dared to dream that I might one day soar into the future with hope and be my best self again. I wondered, "Is joy a discipline of the spirit, even as sadness has become such a comfortable habit, a pervasive attitude of my mind?"

Frankl, who was intimately acquainted with tragedy and suffering, made this bold affirmation, "Even the helpless victim of a hopeless situation, facing a fate he cannot change, may rise above himself, may grow beyond himself, and by so doing change himself. He may turn a personal tragedy into a triumph."[2] When grief at last releases its insistent hold on your heart and mind, you reach a turning point: you begin to think again, clearly and rationally. You realize that you cannot change what happened. You acknowledge that your attitude about the death of a loved one is a choice that is emboldened by your faith. Indeed, it is a choice that is a measure of your faith. At last, you understand that your attitude is fluid, shaped by the spiritual perspective of your grief journey.

As you understand grief better on the upward climb out of the valley of the shadow of death, your renewed confidence will quietly become a positive attitude. You will begin to embrace this fundamental truth: *life is worth living*.

> **Personal Reflections**
> Am I choosing to live in seclusion, isolated and alone?
>
> Am I choosing to blame others, embittered and angry toward those who "caused" (or did nothing to prevent) the death of my loved one?
>
> Am I choosing to torment myself because I could not save his or her life?
>
> Am I choosing to immerse myself in self-pity, in quiet defiance of the world at large?

The explanation of your attitude at this point in your grief journey runs deep. You have loved and been truly loved. If your loss is that of a spouse, perhaps you are among those blessed in life with a soul mate. God-ordained soul mates are like a durable fabric of sturdy weft and warp with threads of trust and respect interwoven at perfect right angles, the complement of vertical to horizontal. Leighton and I were true once-in-a-lifetime soul mates committed to an indestructible partnership. We celebrated each day and lived with passion, as though any moment might be our last. Whatever relationship you have lost in death, you grieve because you have loved and been truly loved.

Because attitude is a choice, when we look into sorrow, we must see not only the emptiness of loss but also the reflection of our own spirits. Be assured that, whomever you have lost, your heart *will* be transformed and your attitude refined as you begin to appreciate that you have given in equal measure your own best gifts to the one who has departed your earthly life. Sometimes this is difficult for us to recognize, but our friends can help us to see the impact we had on the life of our loved one.

Recently I sat at dinner with a friend who remarked on how much I had given to Leighton. I seldom think of any influence or effect I may have had on my husband's life. My memory suggests that he did all the giving. Yet in that moment my spirit lifted, my heart warmed, and my attitude changed as I looked beyond my own sorrow to see from the perspective of another my contribution to Leighton's life.

When you realize that within you shines the eternal, reflected spirit of your loved one, you will want to choose an attitude that forever honors the memory of the one loved and lost to death. This attitude will lift you up and carry you forward into whatever the future may hold. Choosing a new attitude is a biblical mandate:

> *So I tell you this . . . that you must no longer live as the Gentiles do, in the futility of their thinking. They are darkened in their under-standing and separated from the life of God because of the ignorance that is in them due to the hardening of their hearts. . . .*
> *You, however, were taught . . . to put off your old self . . . to be made new in the attitude of your minds; and to put on the new self, created to be like God in true righteousness and holiness.*
> Ephesians 4:17-18, 22-24 NIV

If your heart is intractable and hardened by the pain of death, your grief may well be described as ignorance, futility of thinking, darkness of understanding, and separation from God. Your most powerful response to grief is to put off your old self and be made new in the attitude of your mind. Your old self, like mine, may be a weary, emotionally tattered, half person as familiar to you as a comfortable old bathrobe. But as you grieve, you will discover that you are becoming a different person. Never again will you be the person you once were.

In a sermon, Leighton once said that we will come out of grief different people, and that to be mastered by our grief is unhealthy and unbecoming to a child of God.[3] I have thought about the word *unbecoming*. I remember my grandmother, who lived in a small town in East Texas, using the expression "becoming." With the lilt of a Southern gentlewoman in her voice, she would say with delight, "That's so becoming!" whenever I tried on a new dress she had made for me. It is becoming to a child of God to master not only grief but also the attitude we nurture as we become a new self.

To be made new in the attitude of your mind is to find a new self. You may choose whether you put on your new self and wear it gladly, or whether you shrug into it with reluctance. You may try it on for size and make some adjustments before you are satisfied with the fit. The effect of grief is that it enlarges you to accommodate a new self—a different self, a better self.

In her novel *Adam Bede*, George Eliot wrote these poignant words:

For Adam...had not outlived his sorrow—had not felt it slip from him as a temporary burden, and leave him the same man again. Do any of us? God forbid. It would be a poor result of all our anguish and our wrestling, if we won nothing but our old selves at the end of it—if we could return to the same blind loves, the same self-confident blame, the same light thoughts of human suffering, the same frivolous gossip over blighted human lives, the same feeble sense of that Unknown towards which we have sent forth irrepressible cries in our loneliness. Let us rather be thankful that sorrow lives in us as an indestructible force, only changing its form, as forces do, and passing from pain into sympathy—the one poor word which includes all our best insight and our best love.[4]

A grateful heart has within it the embryo of a new self. The attitude that defines your new self is formed by gratitude for the one you have lost, as well as gratitude for what you have left. Attitude is a choice: "Put off your old self. . .be made new in the attitude of your minds...put on the new self" (Ephesians 4:22-24 NIV).

Personal Reflections
What became of my old self when my loved one died?

How do I put off my old self?

How do I make a "new self" the habit of my mind?

How do I control something as unwieldy and unyielding as my attitude?

How do I manage my attitude?

Courage

We are hard pressed on every side, but not crushed;
perplexed, but not in despair; persecuted, but not
abandoned; struck down, but not destroyed.
2 Corinthians 4:8-9 NIV

The media frequently report a human-interest story of courage and bravery in which the ordinary becomes extraordinary.

- A small child rescues a young sibling.
- Two firefighters pull a driver from a burning car.
- An elderly person is saved from a house fire.
- A vital organ is donated to save the life of another person.
- A pilot safely lands an aircraft in distress, saving the passengers on board.

Courage is heroic and inspiring. The word *courage* derives from the Latin word *cor*, meaning "heart." Courage is your outward response to your inner fear; it is your fear turned inside out. When you respond to grief, you transform fear into courage by doing that which you fear. Then you become stronger. In grief, your challenge is to simultaneously deconstruct fear and reconstruct courage.

At times in grief, you may find that your very will to survive is hard-pressed by grief, yet you are not crushed. When sorrow threatens to overwhelm you, faith in the steadfast love of God fortifies your courage. You may be hard-pressed, but you will not be crushed by grief.

When your loved one dies, you are perplexed by the never-to-be-answered questions about death. For a while, questions may be the constant theme of your chaotic thoughts. You want answers because you are perplexed. In dark moments, you may tiptoe to the precipice of despair and peek over the edge into the darkness of depression, only to behold the vast mystery of death. You are perplexed, but you need not despair.

The following questions are part of the emotional response of your heart to grief. Some of the questions have answers; consider the others with trust and release them in faith.

Personal Reflections
Why?

Why me?

Why didn't God answer my prayers for healing with yes?

Why did this have to happen?

Why did he or she have to die (and not me)?

How can I go on without my loved one?

Some who grieve may feel persecuted or punished by the death of a loved one. Your unresolved emotions, guilt, or a sense of responsibility for what happened may drive the effect of persecution and punishment when someone you love dies. But as you respond to grief, God expands the boundaries of your courage beyond a momentary sense of persecution or punishment. God is with you as you grieve.

God does not punish us. Illness and death are not personal. Yet for months after Leighton died, there was within me a sense of having been punished. For what? For my very humanness? Leighton's illness was the untimely, unexpected interruption of our life together. That felt like punishment to me. But after weeks of struggle, I knew that it was not. Rather, it was what happened to end Leighton's life and that most beautiful part of my life. No one caused it. No one was to blame. It was what happened. It was and is reality, a part of my life forever.

And there is tangible evidence of the self-inflicted wounds of punishment; my emotional scars are proof. They remind me of where I have been. As they have slowly faded and at last blended into the spiritual landscape of my life, the scars of death and grief now intimate healing and wholeness and suggest the future.

No, God does not punish us. God is kind and loving and caring. God forgives us our frailty and weakness and wraps our hurting hearts in love. God does not punish.

If you are unable to function because of your anguish and distress, you may feel struck down for a while. Or you may be physically struck down by unanticipated illness or infirmity. Yet when you courageously rekindle your life from the ashes of sorrow, you acknowledge with gratitude that the death of your loved one has not destroyed you. Life is forever changed, and life will never be the same. Yet you survive. The assurance of life beyond death empowers you to live with courage. You may be struck down, but you are not destroyed.

The spirit that enables you to face difficulty without fear is bravery. Bravery is the bold, intrepid courage inspired by the love of God, who is your citadel and the bastion of your faith. In grief, bravery may be weak and tentative, yet when you dare those conscious acts that test your courage, dividends of self-confidence and hope reward your faith. In his book *The Life Triumphant: Mastering the Heart and Mind,* James Allen writes, "For those who will fight bravely and not yield, there is triumphant victory over all the dark things of life."[5]

Acts of brute courage require bravery to defeat the persistent fears of grief. When you succeed at bravery, you feel as though you deserve a medal or some outward acknowledgment of your courage. You find that your strength is renewed when you courageously venture from your place of pervasive woundedness gradually to rejoin the world.

As I made my way, at first tentatively and then more confidently, through months of arduous grief, new encounters continually stretched me beyond the confines of grief, urgently coaxing me, insisting that I rejoin the world at least where I left it when I succumbed utterly to the heartbreak and overwhelming sorrow of grief. This newfound courage was a challenge of both my fortitude and my faith.

Personal Reflections

Have I returned to church (or somewhere else my loved one and I went regularly together), awkwardly aware of my bravery as I attend without my loved one?

Have I taken a trip without my loved one?

Have I traveled to a familiar or new destination and found the courage to conquer and grow?

Have I had a medical procedure or surgery that was daunting without my loved one at my side?

Have I made the decision to make a major change in life—perhaps tearing out a wall, moving to a new home, or remarriage?

May... God our Father, who loved us and by his grace gave us eternal encouragement and good hope, encourage your hearts and strengthen you in every good deed and word.
2 Thessalonians 2:16-17 NIV

As you respond to grief, you begin to seek the best part of courage: *encouragement*. When you share your grief with others who have experienced the death of a loved one, you recognize that you are not alone. You are encouraged by the gift of community to your grief.

Through my journey of grief, I have come to understand better that the nature of divine love is not to possess but to share, not to control but to free, not to limit but to encourage. On a recent anniversary day, a soul friend wrote these words of encouragement to me: "I have found that sometimes all we can do is wordlessly fall into the abyss of God's love, knowing that God will hold us close and wrap us with his presence and his strength... and somehow we survive those difficult days."

In courage, you are reborn as you slowly find your way back into life. You live again, resurrected from grief. When you receive the promise of eternal encouragement and good hope, you are blessed with comfort and strength, the grace of God's love at work in your life.

Personal Reflections

What fears do I need to express as courage?

Who or what gives me encouragement?

From whom or what do I receive spiritual encouragement?

Can I identify acts of courage that have transformed or could transform my experience of grief?

Victim or Survivor

"For I know the plans I have for you," declares the Lord, "plans to prosper you and not to harm you, plans to give you hope and a future."
Jeremiah 29:11 NIV

On the continuum of responding to grief, the question is whether you want to live as a victim or as a Survivor—capital S. If you consider your attitude and have the courage to change it, you have newfound power because you now understand what you can control and how you control it.

A *victim* is "one that is made to suffer injury, loss, or death."[6] With the death of your loved one, you become a victim through no action of your own. Because death is permanent loss, your life seems irreparably damaged.

You may feel abandoned by God or by the one who died. Indeed, a sense of abandonment is a real part of victimization. You are perhaps unprepared to manage victimization, as I was. You feel helpless to change the effect that death has on your life because your emotional, physical, and spiritual reserves are compromised and depleted by the demands of grief. For a while, you are able to concentrate on nothing except the pain of grief.

> *As he lay sick and dying, Leighton retreated and left me more and more to myself. I was in painful emotional isolation from him, my best friend, my beloved husband. Several months after he died, my grief mentor explained this common occurrence in terminal illness as "tunneling," that is, the one who is dying is unable to cope with anything beyond the present moment of pain and the shadow of the incomprehensible end of life. It is slow resignation and withdrawal into an emotional coma. Leighton descended quickly into illness and could not take me with him into the depths of his unraveling life. He turned inward. I felt that he died to me emotionally before he died physically.*
>
> *I felt abused and angry over his sudden desertion. He was leaving me. I knew that he would never intentionally do or say anything to hurt me. I knew that he loved me. Yet it was so difficult not to personalize the creeping sense of abandonment that grew daily as our tolerance for futility was tried and tested. I did personalize. It did hurt. Admittedly, this was an irrational reaction, yet it was a very human response. Physically, emotionally, and spiritually I felt alone. I was grieving the loss of his beloved spirit to me while he was yet present in life. This "death in life" grief would be ongoing until our final moment of parting.*

Victimization may be a place on the journey through grief where you reside for a while. Author Molly Fumia explains in her book, *Safe Passage,* that when we tenaciously maintain our position as victim, "The temptation is to allow death to claim more than its share, and leave us to our anger and powerlessness."[7] It is important to acknowledge your sense of victimization, but not to succumb to anger or powerlessness, thereby allowing death to claim more than its share of your life on the journey through grief. One way in which you may unintentionally sustain victimization is by allowing social controls to dictate your actions. Social controls insist that you conform to the demands of the society in which you live.

Personal Reflections

Do I betray my grief by putting on a façade that denies my true emotions?

Do I suppress my tears, feigning a smile that belies my broken heart?

Do I feel pressured by others to rejoin life before I have fully engaged with my loss?

Does giving in for the comfort of others feel like giving up on grief?

Yet when circumstances compel you to abandon your victimization before adequately working through your thoughts and feelings about what happened, you forfeit an important part of grief. Someone or something may expect you to function and cope despite your grief, forcing you to live beyond victimization before you have sufficiently honored your grief. For example, you may defer your grief because of the urgency of your job, your children or grandchildren, your aging parents, or any other combination of non-negotiable demands that distract you from your response to grief. The effect may be that you postpone grief for months or even years. Grief can be delayed, but it will not be denied. You are loyal to yourself when you refuse to give up any part of the grief experience necessary for the survival of your soul and spirit.

If you understand what you can control, the following "survival strategies" adapted from a book by grief authors Patsy Brundige and Pat Millican may help you manage victimization in your grief:[8]

- Face being alone.
- Name your thoughts and feelings.
- Allow others to see your tears.
- Ask for help—from family, friends, clergy, or therapist.
- Avoid toxic, angry, or judgmental people and those who want to control.
- Dress and go outside each day.
- Talk to another person each day.

- Move your body; exercise in small ways.
- Eat at least one healthy meal each day.
- Perform only safe tasks that do not exceed your concentration level.
- Avoid excessive use of alcohol and drugs.
- Spend as little money as possible.
- Take care of your health needs because grief impacts the immune system.

Beyond these survival strategies, you respond to grief when you consciously resolve to survive. Your choice is surviving day to day or surviving for life. If we are empowered rather than debilitated by the experience of life and death, we want to survive, to be a Survivor–*capital S.*

At a decisive point along my journey of grief, I began to think, "Is life not more than mere survival? Is my life to be about only long suffering? Has death robbed me of my human capacity for embracing life beyond the pleasure of a cookie?" I would later realize in the hindsight of the road traveled on the journey through grief that all along, survival had been my unstated objective.

When I gave up my own victimhood, I became a serious survivalist. I would not allow those closest to me to confine my life to a smaller version of my inmost self. Choosing to not be limited by others was sometimes painful, yet it was also liberating. It was a subtle, yet powerful turning point in my spiritual maturity through grief. I am a Survivor.

Death forever alters those who survive. You will sense that your identity and your worldview are changing. In grief, you lose not only the one who died but also the person you were when he or she was alive. You lose the assumptions upon which your life was built and your vision of the future. Even as a Survivor you still see the world for a while through a haze of sadness, but ultimately your place in the mainstream of life will come back into view.

Moving from victim to Survivor is a milestone in your response to grief. You begin to recognize this pivotal moment of personal triumph and transformation as you dare to survive in fullness of life. You are a Survivor because you believe and embrace the promise of God's unconditional declaration: "For I know the plans I have for you," declares the LORD, "plans to prosper you and not to harm you, plans to give you hope and a future" (Jeremiah 29:11 NIV).

Personal Reflections

What does it feel like to be a victim?

What does it feel like to be a Survivor?

What are the emotions that describe a victim?

What are the emotions that describe a Survivor?

5

ADJUSTING THROUGH GRIEF

5
ADJUSTING THROUGH GRIEF

The house, our home, is one room too large for me alone. It was our one and only home together. Even now, Leighton's spirit lingers here, at times heavy in the air. There were months of emotional and financial indecision about whether to stay or sell. I debated with myself. Should I stay and make our empty house, once a home filled with love and laughter, into my home? Or should I sell and downsize to something more suited to my needs?

For several months, I busied myself with refreshing and redecorating. The house needed some work, and I thought this might help my spirits. The process both frustrated and awakened my creative energies. It stretched my grief-filled heart and mind to contemplate new life. A friend encouraged me to get a dog, but I would not consider a pet. For months, I could not even buy two pots of geraniums. I would not risk the emotional investment in anything of this world that would surely die.

And so began the emptying of spaces. I donated Leighton's bedding, a sofa, and two chairs to Hurricane Katrina survivors who needed furniture and furnishings. I did not need them, yet I grieved as they left the house because they told a wordless story of a life gone from that place. The vacant, unused room mirrored my soul. I decided to use the empty room to store accessories and odd furniture pieces. There was chaos within; I closed it off from the rest of the house.

Each evening a timer would turn on a lamp, proclaiming that someone was at home. The lamp was my soul in microcosm. A small light, the light of faith, shined within. Amid the clutter was a suggestion that order would someday be restored, that the empty, unused room of my life would again be endowed with meaning and purpose. There was hope that the room would one day be ordered and again inhabited, even as the slow rebirth of my soul from grief signaled a return to fullness of life.

Whenever I passed by Leighton's place at the head of the dining room table, where he sat for family gatherings, I would run my hand through the air as though to touch his sweet head. The pain of this motion several times each day became too cruel. The table, with its mixed memories, was sold and moved on. Months later, I discovered the time-worn linens that adorned the table, useless now with no table to serve.

I bought a used chair. As I carefully cleaned its burnished surface, sanitizing and revitalizing the warm patina, I thought of its connection to someone's living past—and now to someone else's future. My future.

Does it feel at times as if grief defines your life? You may wonder: *Is this who I have become, a half person whose life has context only because of death?* Perhaps your spirit seems resigned to a tentative half life where you live in your mind in a conditioned state of emotional hyper vigilance. You hold on; you let go; you grow forward. You want to live, to have love and joy again flood your life with blessing and abandon, yet the persistent reality of death seems to defy adjustment. Even so, you continue to try to grow forward.

In unexpected pinhole moments, joy beckons to you on the other side of grief, calling you to warm the cold of your heart and live in the moment with joy, enthusiasm, and engagement. You wonder how you will replace your former joy with your loved one gone.

Grief offers you two possibilities: You grow, or you remain rooted in a physical and emotional past that no longer exists. You choose whether to grow and adjust through grief. When you resist growth and adjustment, you succumb to the past, spending your days in frustration and self-pity. But when you choose to grow, you claim life. Growth and adjustment move you to a new place that inspires reinvestment in the future. You grow spiritually when, in faith, you allow the forward dynamic of grief to propel you away from the past toward the light of new life.

The directional arrow on a prominently displayed sign indicates that a neighborhood church has moved a few blocks north. It proclaims, "We've grown. We've moved." Simple words convey the message. With the death of your loved one, something happened and everything changed. Like the words on the sign, your life declares, "I've grown. I've moved." Life continues to unfold when you dare to adjust and grow.

In the following pages, you will move toward greater understanding of some of the personal issues of adjusting through grief. After the death of a loved one, it is always difficult to find where you fit in life. And you will see that this is different for men than it is for women. Finally, you will stretch to adjust to life as it is and soon realize that you have reached acceptance, the springboard for your life ahead.

Where Do I Fit in Life?

Do not worry about anything, but in everything by prayer and supplication with thanksgiving let your requests be made known to God. And the peace of God, which surpasses all understanding, will guard your hearts and your minds in Christ Jesus.
Philippians 4:6-7 NRSV

When you grieve you ask, "Where do I fit in life?" The dangling, pain-filled end of the question implies, "without my loved one." You may be struggling to make sense of life alone without the one loved and lost.

"Where do I fit in life?" may embody much of your anxiety. You may perceive yourself socially as "less than" because of the absence of your loved one. Through attrition, you feel you have been involuntarily demoted to the status of "second-class citizen," which is defined as someone who is not accorded a fair share of respect, recognition, or consideration. When you reject inferior labels, you assert your place in the world, affirming your individuality as you readjust to fit in life.

Recently I observed a distinguished-looking gentleman in a grocery store, a community leader admired for his wealth and social standing, whose wife had died a few months earlier. This titan of industry was clearly overwhelmed, evidently perplexed by the task of shopping. He looked uncomfortable and strangely forlorn. Really, he seemed rather pitiful. Because Leighton had known him personally, I ventured to speak. The man seemed relieved that someone acknowledged that he was not invisible. His entire demeanor suggested the anxiety of a second-class citizen as he attempted to navigate the large, unfamiliar store. Like this man's experience, the death of your loved one may imperil your self-confidence. You may wonder with considerable consternation, "Where do I fit in life?"

As human beings, we want to be treated with respect. When you are suddenly single, you may ask, "Where do I fit in life?"—especially if you are not accorded the same respect as when you were part of a couple. You may feel discounted because of your loss. You also may experience moments of awkwardness if you are invited to join married friends you enjoyed together before the death of your spouse. Or if your child died, and other parents or families invite you to get together, you may feel emotionally excluded because of your loss. Moments when you are the "fifth wheel" accentuate your loss and aloneness. Your comfortable place within the social structure of others has changed because physically you are no longer part of a couple or because a beloved child is no longer alive.

In my own journey of grief, I experienced an inner struggle to move from the defensiveness of grief to the quiet confidence and self-assurance of living forward. I never imagined, never reckoned with, the moment when the worst of grief would be over and behind me, when every breath was not one of sorrow for the one lost to me forever. I reached the other side of the valley of the shadow of death after five laborious years, when grief was an embedded, familiar mode of thinking and being that slowly began to feel stiff and stifling.

This post-grief puberty that challenged me to rediscover myself as a person of stand-alone value and worth was confusing. It stretched me, grew me, and taught me. It was an ongoing test of fortitude and faithfulness. In God's love, my newborn life began, passions reawakening.

Developing your self-perception as a worthwhile stand-alone individual is a formidable hurdle of grief. As you transition through grief, you re-individuate. Or perhaps you truly individuate for the first time in life as you discover your identity without reference to husband or wife, children, siblings, or parents. You appreciate the personal, God-given qualities uniquely your own and explore possibilities beyond your own imagination.

If you have lost your spouse, anxious moments may occur as you adjust to meet the needs of your children. As young children and teens struggle with their own grief, they may demand more of your time and energy. Your role as parent without the equal and opposite presence of your husband or wife is changed and imperceptibly redefined. Rebalancing relationships within a permanently altered family structure is an emotional complication of grief.

With adult children your challenge may be to find the right way to fit into their lives. As they make the effort to include you, they may perceive you as more dependent and in need of a substitute husband or wife, a role you neither desire nor want them to fulfill. You may feel ignored or hurt if they presume on your strength when in fact you need their support. In turn, they may feel inadequate to satisfy your emotional and physical needs. Interpersonal relationships are complicated; each individual family has its own dynamic.

God understands your grief-driven anxiety about your new place in the social structure of life: "Cast all your anxiety on him, because he cares for you" (1 Peter 5:7 NRSV). You may cast off your anxieties for a while, yet as humans, we reserve the right to take them back. Again you may ask, "Where do I fit in life?" When you grieve, it is difficult to relax into God's loving care. Casting is a decisive, conscious act; it is more than just putting aside your anxieties.

If you fish or know someone who does, you have seen firsthand the moment of release that is casting. In one fluid, smooth motion the delicate line soars upward and outward into space. It hovers over the surface for an instant, then floats above it as though suspended in space, and inevitably falls into the water, descending with grace into the unknown depths. Imagine your anxieties on the end of the line, soaring Godward through the air. Casting is letting go, allowing God to calm, relieve, and refresh us when we release our anxieties to God's care.

God promises peace to sustain you as you adjust through grief: "Have no anxiety about anything, but in everything by prayer and supplication with thanksgiving let your requests be made known to God. And the peace of God, which passes all understanding, will keep your hearts and your minds in Christ Jesus" (Philippians 4:6-7 RSV). When you are at peace, restored from within to a life of full citizenship, you again fit into life with renewed strength and rediscovered self-confidence.

Personal Reflections

What are some instances when I have asked, "Where do I fit in life?"

How have I grown through my discovery of where I fit in life?

In what ways do I see myself as a worthwhile, stand-alone individual?

Gender-specific Grief

A *father to the fatherless, a defender of widows,*
is God in his holy dwelling.
Psalm 68:5 NIV

Jesus wept.
John 11:35 NIV

Statistically, women live longer than men do. In our society, there are more widows than widowers.[1] Grief literature and support groups are typically biased toward women; men are remarkably underserved. A mistaken presumption of male grief is that men are brave and strong and do not hurt as much as women.

The Bible includes dozens of verses that refer to widows, usually in the context of care and compassion. Widows were outcasts, left to the mercy of family for their sustenance and livelihood. The book of Ruth is the story of three widows, two young and one old. It relates how they responded to the loss of their husbands, and how God blessed each in a unique way.

The emotional needs of a man with a broken heart are often neglected, especially when a husband survives his wife. There is little reference in the Bible to the grief of men; they were expected to remarry and continue the family lineage after the death of a wife. Widower was a temporary status.

Upon hearing the news that his friend Lazarus died, Jesus was "greatly disturbed in spirit and deeply moved" (John 11:33 NRSV). He was not there when Lazarus died, as he might have been. His emotions were in turmoil; he expressed his pain and sorrow in heartfelt grief: "Jesus wept" (John 11:35 NIV). Jesus showed unqualified emotion as he grieved his friend. The people said, "See how he loved him!" (John 11:36 NRSV).

We know that Jesus was manly. He was a man's man whose primary company was twelve other men. The Bible offers no explanation for his tears and no apology for his outpouring of grief. Love is the universal reason that we grieve.

You love the one who is lost to you in death so intimately and dearly that tears are your purest expression of loss and human pain. Women typically feel comfortable crying—tears of either sadness or joy. In contrast, men are discouraged from tearful self-expression, but men should weep when the heart is broken. They should cry when a beloved person dies and leaves them grieving and perhaps alone. Jesus wept. There is no greater example for men who grieve.

> *One of the special things I cherish about Leighton is that he cried at movies. He was not ashamed to cry and express his emotions.*

For a surviving husband, the death of a wife may result in social disconnection that leads to isolation, loneliness, and depression. This is one of the most difficult aspects of grief for men. Most women have networks for emotional support through family and friends. In a marriage, the wife typically instigates and facilitates most relationships. It is an extra burden of grief for men to sustain meaningful contact with others without their wives.

Many who have lost a spouse struggle with the designations *widow* or *widower*; to some it suggests resignation from life and loss of a future. In the modern world, these words qualify as social controls for those who have experienced the death of a husband or wife; for survivors, these words may feel old-fashioned or dated.

Personal Reflections

Have I been to a doctor's office and filled out a form, confronted by the choice of "widow" or "single"?

What designation would I use to describe my status as living without the one I have loved and lost?

How would I like others to perceive me?

How does the use of *widow* and *widower* affect my attitude and disposition toward grief?

Some women express helplessness or mild resentment about assuming many responsibilities their husbands may have handled exclusively or primarily, such as:

- managing finances
- doing business
- earning a living
- having the car serviced
- keeping the house in repair
- interacting with service providers

Likewise, many practicalities of daily living can be an ongoing struggle for men:

- preparing meals
- eating alone
- doing the laundry
- caring for a house that no longer feels like a home without a wife's loving presence

We... boast in our sufferings, knowing that suffering produces endurance, and endurance produces character, and character produces hope.
Romans 5:3-4 NRSV

This scripture speaks very personally about grief, whether to a man or to a woman. You suffer because you have loved and lost a beloved person in your life;

you endure it because life demands that you live in the present. And after you have suffered for a while, enduring through grief, you are rewarded with fortified character inspired by hope. As men and women of faith, we dare to hope because we believe that in life and in death, and in life beyond death, God is with us. Thanks be to God that we are not alone.

Personal Reflections
What issues of grief are gender-specific for me?

For Men:
Do I allow myself the benefit of tears, or do I repress them?

What is the most difficult aspect of my life without my wife (or other loved one)?

For Women:
What is the most difficult aspect of my life without my husband (or other loved one)?

Adjustment

But this one thing I do: forgetting what lies behind and straining forward to what lies ahead, I press on toward the goal for the prize of the heavenly call of God in Christ Jesus.
Philippians 3:13-14 NRSV

Adjustment often refers to actions accomplished in a single, deft move:

- You adjust the temperature in your home for a comfortable living environment.

- You adjust the setting on the radio or television to assure optimal quality of your entertainment pleasure.
- You adjust the rear- and sideview mirrors of the car before driving.
- You adjust your belt when you overeat.
- You adjust the fit of your clothes when you gain or lose weight.
- You make a claim when your property is damaged; an adjuster estimates the cost of repair.
- You pay taxes on your adjusted gross income.
- You receive a cost-of-living adjustment.

Life is about constant, subtle adjustment. Intuitively you conform to circumstance. God has given you the ability to assess and adapt; you are innately equipped to adjust. Adjustment assumes monumental proportions when you grieve. According to British biologist and philosopher John Mason Tyler, "life is the continual adjustment of internal relations to external relations or conditions."[2] Adjustment is the gradual process that moves us toward acceptance of loss.

Fast-forward adjustment begins with physical debilitation, a terminal diagnosis, or a fatal accident. At once, it may be necessary for you to adjust from a familiar relationship to life bereft of its structure and support, and then again to life as it is. Adjustment is suddenly an intuitive necessity rather than a conscious act.

We sat quietly together in his hospital room the day before his surgery as though it were any other normal Sunday afternoon. Leighton watched golf on television. I read aloud sports news that interested him. He liked being read to; perhaps it reminded him of his mother who read a Bible story to him each night at bedtime when he was a child.

As Sunday ebbed, I prepared to go home for the night. Our parting talk at the end of the day was not particularly meaningful or profound. We prayed together, but my unspoken fear was a force in play that defied all words. I wondered what he was thinking and what he was praying for. I wondered if he was anxious. Did he pray for me and for my strength, or did he assume that it was a resource in endless supply?

I left feeling unsettled because so many words had been left unspoken. We needed more: more time, more communication, more sharing, more peace. At that moment, the consequences of his surgery and its fatal aftermath were simply unimaginable.

> *My worry raged. I feared for him and for myself. I sensed the unalterable changes already happening in my own life. Going home to an empty house was unaccustomed and uncomfortable. I was alone, completely alone without him. Our world was ending, and I was powerless to stop it. I ferociously resisted inevitable adjustment to utter chaos and irreversible circumstance.*

What makes your adjustment so difficult? American philosopher Eric Hoffer affirms, "We have to adjust ourselves, and every radical adjustment is a crisis in self-esteem."[3] You have spent all or part of your life in a relationship physically dissolved by the event of death. In order to adjust, you are forced to change yourself in a variety of ways. Perhaps you . . .

- adjust to the absence of the one who is gone.
- adjust to a home that seems suddenly silent and empty; you turn to speak and no one is there.
- experience a void where you have listened and been heard.
- adjust to physical aloneness when life has been inextricably entwined with another.
- miss the companionship and partnership of your loved one.
- adjust to the reality of daily life.
- eat alone.
- provide for yourself.
- are your own caregiver.
- learn new modalities of independence.
- learn how to function without your loved one.
- adjust your self-perception as you go into the world alone.
- learn more about confidence, courage, and self-affirmation.
- adjust to the role of sole parent or grandparent to your children, fulfilling the role of mother and father or grandmother and grandfather.
- endow future generations with a shared legacy of love and generosity.
- adjust to personal management of your finances, health, and social interaction with others.

For a while, you hold on desperately to all that has passed away from your life. Your struggle to adjust may be a stubborn defense of the past, reluctance to embrace the present, or obstruction of hope for the future.

Many months after Leighton's death, I questioned whether I was ready to move forward, to dare and dream that life would be better. I struggled on the threshold of the present, drawn toward the past, not wanting to let go of any part of "us," yet straining toward some future, a future of hope and a return of joy to my life. I knew that the past is a place of reference, not a place of residence; that what happened was in the past; that both living in defense of the past and living defensively in the present negate the defenseless future.

Here and now are the coordinates of the present. I knew I could not hang onto a past that would never be the present again. That was then; this is now. By its very omission, it is profound that Romans 8:38-39 does not include the past as a force capable of separating us from the love of Christ: "For I am convinced that neither death, nor life ... nor things present, nor things to come ... will be able to separate us from the love of God in Christ Jesus our Lord" (NRSV).

Adjustment is stretching; it is the discovery that you are more resilient than you imagine. Slowly you realize that you can let go and hold on at the same time in one seamless emotional stand. "Everything old has passed away; see, everything has become new!" (2 Corinthians 5:17 NRSV). In her book *Safe Passage*, Molly Fumia writes, "We hold onto memories, and we let them go; we hold onto feelings, and we let them go. We hold onto an old way of being, because the self we still are resides there, and we let go to a new way of being, so that the self can live on."[4]

Personal Reflections

What old things seem "passed away" from my life because of the death of my loved one?

Have some of my pre-grief relationships "passed away"?

Are people, places, or experiences from my life together with my loved one now part of the past—"passed away" from my life?

It was two years after Leighton's death before I began to feel that somewhere below the grief-weary surface of my soul there was a fountain of joy waiting to spring forth, reawakening me to delight, pleasure, happiness, and joy. I held on, waiting. I wanted to believe that life would again be rich and full and content with soul-saturating peace.

As you adjust through grief, you will slowly let go of the physical life that once was. But you will never forget, ever. Your earthly life together was real. Nothing can void or erase what you experienced in your lifetime together with your loved one, however long or short. What lies behind is your history; it is part of who you will yet become. The past informs the rest of the life you have been given to live. You cherish the unforgettable, build on the past, and hold on to all that gives value and worth to life, conformed to the reality of the present.

In his book *The Inner Voice of Love: A Journey Through Anguish to Freedom,* Henri Nouwen wrote,

> You will see that you are no longer there: the past is gone, the pain has left you, you no longer have to go back and relieve it, you no longer depend on your past to identify yourself.... From the perspective of the life you now live and the distance you now have, your past does not loom over you. It has lost its weight and can be remembered as God's way of making you more compassionate and understanding toward others.[5]

"But this one thing I do: forgetting what lies behind and straining forward to what lies ahead, I press on toward the goal for the prize." (Philippians 3:13-14 NRSV). Within adjustment lies the promise that there is yet life for which to strain forward, that something does lie ahead. There is a goal; there is a prize with notes of joy and possibility. Though it may seem so for a while, you did not die physically when your loved one died. Your purpose and destiny did not die with the one who is gone.

After Leighton died, I understood better why joy was so elusive. Leighton and I lived on the mountaintop of sustained joy every day for eighteen years. We were a matched pair, masculine and feminine sides of the same coin made of the purest, most refined gold—that of true love. We were one. His love made me real; my love made him real. A part of me—the part brimming with love and joy for him, for life, and for the future—died a hard and bitter death over the course of his illness. And when he died, it seemed that my joy died.

Growing through grief is the slow work of constant adjustment. As you adjust, you reanimate to life. Like a thoroughbred racehorse running full out for the finish line, you press on toward the goal for the prize, straining forward toward new life. When you relax into the future with faith, you claim the prize of the high calling of God for life today, tomorrow, and evermore.

Personal Reflections
What are the challenges of adjustment for me?

What crises of self-esteem am I experiencing?

How do I hold on and let go at the same time?

Acceptance

We know that in everything God works for good with those who love him,
who are called according to his purpose.
Romans 8:28 RSV

As you journey through grief, you follow the path through the valley of the shadow of death. First, you descend its depths; then, slowly but surely, you ascend, always moving toward acceptance. Yet on the way to acceptance, you perhaps pause for a moment to take a final backward glance. You remember the dark sadness, sorrow, and emotional turmoil of compelling grief that once held you captive. On the other side of grief, at last you see clearly where you have been and what you have been through. You complete the journey because you have dared to travel this lonely, deserted road of the heart.

> *Knowing that the acceptance of death was the doorway to a new life for me, I questioned whether I wanted to walk over that threshold and leave the grim parts of my life-altering experience behind. The death of my beloved husband was catastrophic, tragic, and entirely personal. My living rock is gone forever. It is life without his hand in mine, his soul lighting my way each day with its joy and goodness, that has been so difficult to accept. The daily challenge continues to be seeking the light of his spirit rather than abiding in the darkness of his death.*

Acceptance is a slow metamorphosis; it is the emotional maturing of your adjustment to life as it is becoming. When adjustment becomes the norm, you move resolutely toward acceptance. You accept that your loved one is physically gone and acknowledge this as permanent. You understand what happened and know that the outcome cannot be changed. Though you do not like it, reluctantly, you accept it. As you have so faithfully done with grief, you work at acceptance. Perhaps you are able to time-date a moment of acceptance, or acceptance may simply occur. You near acceptance when you at last acknowledge that you are no longer actively grieving.

If you allow grief to defeat your spirit, acceptance may be dull resignation. Grace, courage, and wisdom are the hallmarks of acceptance. Protestant theologian Reinhold Niebuhr is attributed as the author of the well-known serenity prayer:

> *God, give us grace to accept with serenity the things that cannot*
> *be changed, courage to change the things that should be changed,*
> *and the wisdom to distinguish the one from the other.*[6]

In acceptance, you transcend physical loss and embrace the spirit of that person's life and love that remains with you always. In *Transcending Loss,* psychotherapist and grief counselor Ashley Davis Prend states, "Death doesn't end the relationship, it simply forges a new type of relationship—one based not on physical presence but on memory, spirit, and love."[7] As adjustment slowly shifts to acceptance, the cold reality of absence is eased by the certainty of enduring love: "Love and faithfulness meet together, righteousness and peace kiss each other. Faithfulness springs forth from the earth, and righteousness looks down from heaven" (Psalm 85:10-11 NIV). The whispered spiritual presence of your loved one surrounds you each day, encouraging you to live on and share your legacy of love. The core of acceptance is indwelling—the indwelling of the love of your deceased loved one and the indwelling of the love of God.

O God, you have saved my life through these years of acute grief and sorrow. As, more and more, I accept the death of my beloved, I understand better your abiding love and grace in my heart. I listen, and you ask me to trust you with all of my large and loving heart. Yes, this is who I am without the mantle of grief suffocating my spirit. I have faith that you have a plan for me, a plan with hope and a future. Thank you for your indwelling love.

We know that in everything God works for good with those who love him, who are called according to his purpose.
Romans 8:28 RSV

You may believe with certainty that God works *in* everything *for* good *with* those who love God, who are called according to God's purpose. Yet you may question, as I did, how the death of your loved one can possibly be for good in your life. The case for acceptance lies within the prepositions: *in* everything God works *for* good, *with* those who love God.

- God has not ordained your loss and sorrow. Rather, God meets you at your place of brokenness; God is there *in* everything.
- God uses grief to teach you more of God's faithfulness and steadfast love. God works *for* good, using that which has changed your life to promote deeper, more profound faith.
- God works *with* you because you are called according to God's purpose, that is, because you have faith in God's plan for your life. God leads you and works *with* you to shape a life of meaning and purpose.

Everything new is an outward reflection of your growing acceptance. If you buy sheets, decide on a new car, take a trip, or move your place of residence, you affirm acceptance of life as it is. Within the balance of loss and acceptance, equalized by a more mature faith, your heart urges you to live forward.

Finally, acceptance is victory. It is the strength and power of an unconquerable soul. As clouds of doubt and fear slowly drift away, you stand at last in the radiance of full sunlight, assured from within that there is life beyond grief because there is life after death.

Personal Reflections

What is my experience of God's good at work in my life?

Have I reached the moment of acceptance? If so, when did it happen?

Have I yet consciously realized that I am no longer actively grieving?

What are the hallmarks of acceptance for me—or what do I anticipate them to be?

6
MOVING FORWARD IN GRIEF

6
MOVING FORWARD IN GRIEF

In my journey through grief there came that unexpected moment when I could no longer elude an unmistakable cue for rejoining life in its fullness. I knew that this did not mean that the work of grief was complete, for there is no finite end to grief. Was this impetus, then, an illusion, one easily defeated by the habit of hopelessness? I held back, reluctant to trust and embrace this life that is mine. Did I cherish continued existence as the inhabitant of an empty shell? No, I knew that life is not for living on the half-shell. In that conscious moment of feeling more self-confident and again present to myself, changed after a long and precarious absence from the world, I responded to the irresistible emotional urge to engage and venture forth again.

It happened when I reached out to encounter a stranger for even a moment, testing to see if there was still a heart within to validate the mechanics of a long-unused smile. It was when I began to thirst to be refilled by the adventure of life, to rediscover vitality after a long and arduous journey. It was that moment when I felt like wearing my red shoes again.

When Leighton and I left our wedding reception on the balmy April day we were married, I wore red shoes, both a fashion statement and perhaps my own small statement of life and joy. Now I was reconsidering wearing my red shoes again. I looked and touched. They drew me in, yet I could not commit. Had old things passed away? Or was everything becoming new?

My red shoes were a metaphor or symbol for renewed life. Perhaps you, too, have—or will have—a metaphor or symbol for renewed life. You know that you are near the end of the journey through the valley of the shadow of death when you begin to reengage fully with life and move forward in your grief.

A few questions perhaps may be unresolved for you, but most likely you are down the road on your journey through grief. You look ahead, eager to move away from grief and back into life. You believe there is a future. You sense that life is becoming more hope-filled. You dare to entertain the idea of joy. You pray for strength to be in the world, because you are changed and curiously fortified. You have been through and survived the experience of grief. You now understand grief. You reach out to life. You dare to move forward.

In the following pages, you will consider the answer to a concluding question of grief—one that many who grieve want to know: How long does grief last? You also will see that as you continue the journey and move forward, the final "events" of grief are healing and your intentional reinvestment in happiness and hope.

How Long Does Grief Last?

I tell you the truth, you will weep and mourn while the world rejoices.
You will grieve, but your grief will turn to joy.
John 16:20 NIV

How long does grief last? The answer to this question of grief is an ongoing discovery as you confront and resolve your own personal issues. Grief does not follow the calendar; it is not a straight-line experience. Grief comes and it goes; it ebbs and it flows. Imperceptibly, you learn to live alongside grief, but it usually lasts longer than most who grieve expect, for grief will not be rushed. Poet Henry Taylor wrote, "He that lacks time to mourn, lacks time to mend."[1]

The infrastructure of life consists of both beginning and end. Like me, perhaps you, too, want to control the "when" of both the beginning and the end of most things in life. Because grief is your emotional reaction to the event of death, its onset and end are unique and individual. Each person starts at a different point. For example, grief may have had its beginning as an undertow that swelled through stages of illness, crashing onto the shore of your well-ordered life as the end of life neared. Whatever the circumstance, when and how grief begins may affect how long grief lasts.

Because grief defies an exact moment, your instinct may be to ignore it rather than to enter into it. Some who have experienced the death of a loved one choose simply to hang on mindlessly until grief is over. In fact, you do not enter into grief. Grief enters into you. You move from "Why did this happen?" to "How will I go on?" You experience disbelief and shock and then the reality of life without your loved one. As the forward dynamic of life gradually redirects your grief, you become more immersed in the positive, life-sustaining memories of your relationship with your loved one than in the unalterable fact of death. For some, it may take several years to work through profound loss and grief—the kind of "no end in sight" emotional turmoil that requires the insight of a professional. For others, there may be a defining moment, such as remarriage, that clearly signifies the end of grief. Because your emotions do not conform to life's infrastructure, the end of grief is personal. How long your grief lasts is an intimate process of self-determination. You grieve as long as you grieve.

Each year on the anniversary of September 11, 2001, the enduring grief of those whose loved ones died on that fateful day is once again compelling. A few years ago on the sixth anniversary, a reporter for the *New York Times* wrote an article that implied that "by now," six years after the event that changed all of life forever, survivors should be over the worst of their grief and therefore should be willing to scale down the annual public commemoration of that horrible day. In the article, the reporter quoted a nursing supervisor who used the term "shelf life" in reference to the survivors' grief.[2] This rather callous journalistic suggestion, rife with implied judgment, questions the validity and duration of individual grief. The survivors of 9/11 will always grieve. The premise that there is a "shelf life" for grief denies the most solemn and personal aspect of death: *you must grieve in order to live.*

You may ask, "Is there a 'shelf life' for grief?" For anyone who has experienced death in the first person, the answer is assuredly no. Figuratively, you may box up and shelve your unresolved issues for a while. But some time later, from the improved perspective of time, you probably will decide to take down the box and revisit its content. You may look through what is there and touch it again. Perhaps you will hold it close and reexamine it. You may decide to let it go or hold onto it and put it back on the shelf. Or you may decide to file it, put it in another box of odds and ends, shred it, scrap it, or put it on a figurative bonfire and burn it. This is the only real "shelf life" that pertains to grief. Unlike well-marked packages at a supermarket, grief has no expiration date.

Although it is not usually so, in some instances grief may last a lifetime. Queen Victoria made a public and private career of long-term grief as the eternal widow of Windsor. In 1840, Victoria married her mother's nephew Albert, who, as husband and prince consort, was the center of her life. He was her confidant, friend, and advisor. They were married twenty-one years and had nine children. When he died in 1861, Victoria was only forty-two.

The Queen's grief was profound. She did not appear in public for three years and wore mourning clothes for over ten years. Her subjects thought her response to death exaggerated, shocking, and abnormal because she would not be moved from her grief. An entire nation expected her to abandon her grief and "get on with life."

When she emerged from her self-imposed seclusion, Victoria felt her return to public life was a betrayal of her husband. She suffered from chronic, prolonged depression, and was physically crippled by her grief. Yet she lived another forty years as queen and empress of a vast empire. She never recovered; she grieved without apology or explanation until she died. Victoria grieved for a lifetime; there was no "shelf life" to her grief.

"I tell you the truth, you will weep and mourn while the world rejoices. You will grieve, but your grief will turn to joy" (John 16:20 NIV). Though you have no instructions on how long your grief will last or how long you should grieve, your assurance is that grief will turn to joy.

- Grief turns to joy when your life blossoms in unexpected ways, bringing renewal and hope for the future.
- Grief turns to joy in moments that celebrate the life and love of your loved one.
- Grief turns to joy with the birth of a child or grandchild.
- Grief turns to joy with a new companion for the rest of life's journey.
- Grief will turn to joy when at last you reunite with the one you have grieved in life and in death.

Toward the end of my journey through grief, my spirit wanted to "start fresh," to dare to hope that I might again live in joy. I longed to rejoice, to be glad, to have a new song in my heart, to give up my fear, to take on trust, and to spend the rest of my life in gratitude.

I came to realize that grief is not merely enduring until something changes; it is triumphing over tragedy, loss, and in the end, grief itself. My inner struggle in and with life went on as I continued to stretch and grow spiritually. My life was damaged but not permanently disabled by Leighton's death. I stretched toward the open road of life—a way of hope, surprise, and, at the last, joy.

So, how long does grief last? Grief lasts as long as it lasts.

Healing

He heals the brokenhearted,
and binds up their wounds.
Psalm 147:3 NRSV

Is there healing *in* grief? Is there healing *from* grief? The best analogy is the human body. Physical injury causes a wound of finite, reparable damage that can be treated with expectation of healing. Death wounds the human soul and spirit; it causes you to grieve. For some, the wound is immeasurable—so deep that healing seems impossible. For others, the wound is less severe. The greater the love for the one you have loved and lost, the larger and deeper your wound.

As with any physical injury, we must take seriously the wound of grief. Honest, accurate assessment facilitates its treatment, both mentally and spiritually. For many, the wound is caused by slow leave-taking after months or years of chronic illness. For others, death is a tragic, gaping wound in need of immediate, acute care. Your own unresolved circumstances may compound your trauma:

- The unexpected onset of disease when your loved one seemed otherwise healthy.
- The rapid demise of your loved one.
- The affliction, pain, and suffering caused by a disease that could not be treated or conquered.
- The event of accident or sudden death.
- The loss of control in life.

As with the body, you treat your wound with constructive pain relievers:
- Work
- Church
- Community service/voluntarism
- Hobbies
- Recreation
- Travel
- Children, grandchildren, friends

In your moments of acute woundedness, you may have tried to anesthetize your pain with easy remedies (alcohol, food, medication), yet likely you have found that this does not work. Quick cures seldom last. God is the one true source of reconstructive relief from the pain of your grief: "He heals the brokenhearted, and binds up their wounds" (Psalm 147:3 NRSV).

Relentless, unremitting grief is an infection that can invade the wounds of your soul. When grief permanently overwhelms you, it destroys your very will to live. If your grief is tenacious, spiritual healing begins only when you affirm that you want to be made well and that you want your journey through grief to be over. In her book *Safe Passage,* Molly Fumia writes, "Healing is not a wish that can be granted by someone else. It is a well within us that we alone can tap. It is a desire that we allow for, in our own time, by our own choosing."[3]

When you are injured, wound dressings are carefully applied to your physical body to promote healing and protect the point of invasion from germs. Similarly, in grief you may slap a figurative bandage on your wound, not so much to promote healing but to protect yourself from additional hurt and pain. Because you may sense that others do not want to see the gaping hole in your spirit—the imperfect part of your life that is grief—you cover it up with a self-styled emotional wound dressing.

- For friends, your bandage may be decorated with ridiculous yellow happy faces that considerately distract them from your grief.
- For children and grandchildren, your bandage is perhaps a "tough strip," designed to be both protective and impervious.
- For others, you perhaps disguise your woundedness with a clear bandage that conceals your hurt yet does not make your injury truly invisible.
- If you are indifferent to appearance, perhaps you apply a clumsy bandage of gauze and tape that is just "good enough."
- Or perhaps you abandon convention altogether and grieve openly, your gaping emotional wound uncovered and visible for all to see.

Assuming that there is some improvement, you risk the smart of momentary pain when your bandage is ripped from the skin—ouch! Likewise, when inevitable remembrance days tear away the protective covering of your grief wound, you are reminded that you are still vulnerable to pain. When your wound is reopened and exposed by occasions and events, you examine the damage and gratefully discern that you are healing from the inside. You realize that revisiting a painful moment is not a complete re-injury; rather, it is a brief uncovering that requires only the fresh bandage of a new day.

Healing is not linear. There is no timeline or prescribed cure date for grief. Healing is the gradual process of becoming whole or sound. When you at last take off your protective bandage and find that you are well, you see healing both within and without.

Spiritual and emotional healing from grief are perhaps better described as *recovery*. To recover is to "convalesce . . . forge ahead . . . get better . . . grow . . . overcome . . . pull through . . . recuperate . . . restore . . . start anew."[4] If you are finding satisfaction in life with renewed self-confidence, then you are recovering. Likely, you have heard yourself say, whether silently or aloud, "I am better," "I want to live," "Life is good," or some other self-talk that is affirmative and positive. This is a sure indication that you are recovering from grief.

As with the physical body, there is a scar forever in your soul to remind you of your grief. It is at first red and tender, and then slowly it fades until it is almost invisible. It is a medical fact that scar tissue becomes the strongest part of your body. As your spirit and heart slowly mend, you become strongest in your broken places—within the very fiber of your soul. The scar, a spiritual and emotional reminder of your most acute pain, is now part of who you are. Your scar affirms the best part of your own immortality, your soul. Though you are wounded by the death of a beloved person in your life, you are healed by God's triumphant adequacy: "He heals the brokenhearted, and binds up their wounds" (Psalm 147:3 NRSV).

Personal Reflections

How long does it take to heal? How long do I think it will take for me to heal?

When will I know that I am healed?

How will I know that I am healed?

Renewing Spirit, come breathe through us with hope that heals,
with faith that thrills;

. . . .

So may your gifts of grace increase to send us forth in love and peace.
"We Come, O Christ," Carl P. Daw Jr. (1944-)[5]

Happiness

"Blessed are those who mourn, for they will be comforted."
Matthew 5:4 NRSV

As your grief progresses beyond the pain of loss and loneliness, you may ask yourself, "Will I ever be happy again?" Like me, you might answer, "I might be happy again if only something would change so that everything would be better"—a thought that denies the reality of grief.

"Blessed are those who mourn, for they will be comforted" is the fourth beatitude or "declaration of blessedness" from the Sermon on the Mount (see Matthew 5:1-12). This counterintuitive promise assures you that because you mourn, you will be *blessed*—or, in some translations, *happy*. The connection between blessedness and happiness lies within the word *beatitude,* from the Latin *beatitudo* ("state of blessedness"), *beatus* ("happy, blessed"), and *beare* ("to make happy").

You may struggle to reconcile blessedness and mourning, happiness and grief. You may want to look at it this way: because you mourn, you are comforted; when you are comforted, you are blessed. Because mourning is the expression of your inmost sorrow, grief insists that you mourn before you are blessed with authentic comfort and happiness.

What is happiness? The root of the word happiness is *hap*, which means "fortune or chance."[6] It occurs in words of both positive and negative connotation: happening, mishap, haphazard, and happenstance. The unstated meaning of happiness is that chance or fortune determines your state of being—that you are not entirely in charge of your own happiness.

For some, happiness is a way of life. Those with a naturally sunny disposition often sustain a greater sense of hope and optimism through grief than those who are by nature more introverted or reserved.

In her best-selling book *Eat, Pray, Love,* Elizabeth Gilbert writes:

> People universally tend to think that happiness is a stroke of luck or something that will maybe descend upon you like fine weather if you're fortunate enough. But that's not how happiness works. Happiness is the consequence of personal effort. You fight for it, strive for it, insist upon it, and sometimes even travel around the world looking for it. You have to participate relentlessly in the manifestations of your own blessings. And once you have achieved a state of happiness, you must never become lax about maintaining it, you must make a mighty effort to keep swimming upward into that happiness forever, to stay afloat on top of it.[7]

Happiness, then, is the reward. It is the result of something you have already done: you have mourned. Happiness comes to you by indirection: "Blessed are those who mourn, for they will be comforted" (Matthew 5:4 NRSV).

Happiness is the by-product of your inner stability rather than your outward security. When you grieve, you explore and discover, perhaps for the first time in life, the depth of your inner stability. Although death affects your sense of well-being, you are not wholly at the mercy of happenstance or outward circumstance. Rather, happiness is the triumph of your inner stability over your outward security.

Often quiet desperation, loneliness, and emotional misery drive the pursuit of superficial happiness. The media suggest every day what will make you happy. Family and friends want to reconstruct your happiness according to *their* idea of your well-being. But the truth is that happiness comes only from within. Happiness is an inside story. It begins where you are; it happens from within your heart.

Personal Reflections
What makes me happy?

When am I happy?

Do I have the inner stability to live a life of sustained happiness? Why or why not?

Seventeenth-century English essayist Joseph Addison wrote, "Three grand essentials to happiness in this life are something to do, something to love, and something to hope for."[8] As life unfolds, happiness may be more about cause and effect. Though you still may be lonely from time to time, at last you grow accustomed to being alone. Life slowly flourishes with renewed energy that begins to feel like happiness. If what you experience is not exactly happiness, then perhaps a quiet contentment that honors the joyful memory your loved one.

A life of service is the secret to happiness. Speaking with a group of children, Albert Schweitzer is reported to have said, "I don't know what your destiny will be but one thing I know, the only ones among you who will be really happy are those who have sought and found a way to serve."[9]

The happy person is one who comforts because she has been comforted, one who loves because he has been loved, and one who finds life in giving it away. In giving, you receive; in selflessness, you find. This is authentic happiness.

Spiritual happiness is only a small step away from joy, the ultimate quest of your grief journey. Joy is the balance of peace and hope that resides deep within your heart. "Blessed are those who mourn, for they will be comforted" (Matthew 5:4 NRSV).

My life flows on in endless song;
Above earth's lamentation,
I catch the sweet, tho' far-off hymn
That hails a new creation;

Through all the tumult and the strife,
I hear the music ringing;
It finds an echo in my soul—
How can I keep from singing?

What tho' my joys and comfort die?
The Lord my Saviour liveth;
What tho' the darkness gather round?
Songs in the night He giveth;
No storm can shake my inmost calm,
While to that refuge clinging;
Since Christ is Lord of heaven and earth.
How can I keep from singing?

I lift my eyes; the cloud grows thin;
I see the blue above it;
And day by day this pathway smooths,
Since first I learned to love it;
The peace of Christ makes fresh my heart,
A fountain ever springing;
All things are mine since I am His—
How can I keep from singing?

"How Can I Keep from Singing?" Robert Lowry (1826-1899)[10]

Hope

But this I call to mind, and therefore I have hope: The steadfast love of the
LORD never ceases; his mercies never come to an end; they are
new every morning; great is your faithfulness.
"The Lord is my portion," says my soul,
"therefore I will hope in him."
Lamentations 3:21-24 ESV

Hope is the teaser of headlines. You read the paper expecting good news, yet often the story belies real hope. Without hope, life is bland and uninspired. Hope is the salt that flavors your life; hope is the seasoning that adds spice to your expectation of life.

Hope does not erase the reality of death or the toll it takes. When life implodes, you are assaulted on every side. Death happens, but it is not final. Death has robbed you of a loved one's companionship, but it can never rob you of his or her love—nor can it rob your loved one of yours.

Grief need not be a place of emotional surrender and existential catastrophe. It can be the most honest, whole, and faithful place you can possibly stand and find hope. When hope feels like tentative renewal, life may still feel rather lukewarm and tepid. This momentary state of suspended animation is a quiet phase, a readying, resting, regrouping after the long grief journey. Breathe, relax, rest, live—one day at a time. Hope.

Hopelessness is the dark underside of grief. Grief assails your hope; without hope, you despair. When you despair, you drift into cynical acceptance or defeated resignation. I struggled with the dark specter of hopelessness through much of my own journey through grief.

On the periphery of my daily route to and from the hospital for eight weeks was a homeless man whose small, wasted body testified to chronic alcohol and drug abuse. Day after day, he squatted in the shade of an underpass, balanced against the silver pole of a street sign, a pile of cigarette butts in the space between his splayed knees. He held no sign, no stained empty coffee cup, and no hat for donations. He did not openly solicit, but his overwhelming pathos was its own silent entreaty for help. We did not make eye contact—his world of oblivion remote from the dire dailiness of mine. When I tried to give him a bottle of water, the traffic light changed too quickly. Impatient motorists at the precarious intersection where he sat on his thin haunches day in and day out impelled me reluctantly forward. I added to a growing list of personal failures my inability to extend simple outreach to one so obviously in need.

I saw him in that urban landscape every day; I wondered where he slept and how he ate. Unprotected by a grimy baseball cap, his sun-burned face suggested exposure to the extremes of that hot summer. His vacant, alcoholic stare focused on some nothingness a million miles away. He was there, yet so far away. I thought about his life. He was someone's son, someone's brother, perhaps a husband or father. This daily intimate glimpse into the life of another was detached yet pro-foundly personal. Our anonymous bond demanded that he have a name. For no particular reason, I decided it was Tom. I looked for Tom every day, faithfully at his proprietary spot as I faithfully came and went.

The essence of my voyeuristic kinship to Tom was our shared hopelessness. His tattered, overexposed exterior was the reflection of my life at the edge of impending disaster. Tom embodied my own empty helplessness as certain destruction advanced toward the epicenter of my life.

Then one day, road construction changed the area, and I never saw him again. If he died, there was no obituary notice for this strange companion of my coming and going.

Though everything seemed, in fact, hopeless, I did not utterly succumb. At times it felt almost impossible to hope, yet I knew in faith that there is always hope in God.

> "Why are you downcast, O my soul,
>   Why so disturbed within me?
> Put your hope in God,
>   for I will yet praise Him
>   My Savior and my God." (Psalm 42:5-6 NIV)

Hope leaves no room for despair.

Hope is more than an emotion. You hope because you are a divinely created human being. No matter how dire or hopeless the circumstances of impending death, you continue to hope. Even if your loved one is hopelessly ill, you continue to hope because you cannot imagine imminent death or how your life will be beyond the death of the one you love. Irish writer and playwright Oliver Gold-smith wrote these words: "Hope, like the gleaming taper's light, adorns and cheers our way. And still, as darker grows the night, emits a brighter ray."[11]

Hope is the conviction that the desirable is obtainable and that events will turn out for the best. Hope implies perseverance, the belief that a positive outcome is possible even in the face of evidence to the contrary.

The aftermath of Leighton's death left me feeling haunted. I was a reluctant survivor with guilt and inner turmoil. I needed to understand what caused his medical demise and death. After weeks of mental preoccupation with the reconstruction of events, I realized that I could not move on from our experience until I confronted the hospital. I needed a personal encounter with someone "in charge" to articulate our victimization during the eight weeks of Leighton's post-surgery illness.

I had no real expectation of institutional accountability or responsibility. I was not naïve. However, my mission was clear. I wanted to advocate for others. There must be some redemptive value in Leighton's death. My premise was that if even one patient or family lacking financial, emotional, or spiritual resources could benefit from improvement in the hospital by confronting the behemoth institution, Leighton's tragic death would not have been in vain. I knew I must do what I could to help myself out of the abyss of circular questions that were my daily monologue of self-recrimination. I met with administrators. I talked; they listened.

Only another patient will know whether my effort was of any benefit, whether any changes were made, or whether anyone paused for even a moment to consider or reassess the issues of compassion and humanity in the care of patients and their families.

At the time, I thought my effort probably did not produce results. Yet in December 2008, a powerful series of articles entitled "At the Edge of Life" by Lee Hancock appeared in the Dallas Morning News. *The subject was care for people and families facing life-threatening conditions. I read on, gripped by the powerful suggestion, the intimation, indeed, the idea that my effort to advocate—despite or perhaps because of my broken heart—made a difference. I looked at every face in every photo and somehow realized that I was a part of the picture for insisting that our story be heard by someone "in charge."*

In the article, places and people who had participated in my conversations with administrators were referenced. I dared to hope that our experience had made a difference. We do not know how our lives intersect. I desperately needed to believe that there was redemptive value in Leighton's horrible illness and dying, in our story of life and death. God is at work in the world, in God's perfect timing, unknown and unseen to us. Our job is to trust and hope.

Hope is based in reality...

- Hope is not naïve optimism.
- Hope is not wishful thinking.
- Hope is not a positive attitude.
- Hope is not a passive wish or dream.

Hope is your fear defeated. The hope of your grief is confidence in the divine plan of a loving, caring God—the author of all hope. "Now hope that is seen is not hope. For who hopes for what is seen? But if we hope for what we do not see, we wait for it with patience" (Romans 8:24-25 NRSV). In the will to hope, we find the strength to live and the courage to die.

We are to "rejoice in hope, be patient in suffering, persevere in prayer" (Romans 12:12 NRSV). The most active form of your hope is expressed in prayer. As the scripture says, "The widow who is really in need and left all alone puts her hope in God and continues night and day to pray and to ask God for help" (1 Timothy 5:5 NIV). In prayer, you entrust the most fervent desires of your heart to God because you desire restoration to life. You hope because you have faith.

Hope, then, is sacred evidence of expectancy, patience, trust, and faith. "In this life we have three great lasting qualities—faith, hope and love. But the greatest of them is love" (1 Corinthians 13:13 JBP). If you think about it, hope stands in the middle—its bookends are faith and love. What God has done through faith, hope, and love illuminates what God will do. Hope does not rely on your own aspirations but on God. You hope for the future because the future belongs to God. "And hope does not disappoint us, because God has poured out his love into our hearts by the Holy Spirit" (Romans 5:5 NRSV).

In bold declaration of faith, affirm that hope does not disappoint you, for in God, the best is yet to be.

Be strong and take heart,
all you who hope in the LORD.
Psalm 31:24 NIV

May the God of hope fill you with all joy and peace as you trust in him,
so that you may overflow with hope by the power of the Holy Spirit.
Romans 15:13 NIV

Happy are those...
whose hope is in the LORD their God.
Psalm 146:5 NRSV

May your unfailing love rest upon us, O LORD,
even as we put our hope in you.
Psalm 33:22 NIV

Personal Reflections
What do I hope for in life?

What inspires my hope?

Is my hope based in reality or fantasy?

Do I have the spiritual resolve to hope again for a life that is full, even without my loved one?

7

GROWING SPIRITUALLY THROUGH GRIEF

7
GROWING SPIRITUALLY THROUGH GRIEF

About two miles from where I grew up there was a Mrs. Baird's bakery. The location of this behemoth factory was an urban anomaly for Dallas, Texas. It bordered an upscale residential neighborhood across from Southern Methodist University on the southwest corner of Mockingbird Lane and State Highway 75.

In full-page newspaper ads on November 2, 1953, Mrs. Baird invited the city to attend the opening of the new bakery. At the time, it was the world's largest automated bread factory. The announcement encouraged the public to bring the whole family and wear their walking shoes for the quarter-mile tour.

And so on a balmy Friday evening in the spring of 1954, we took the tour to see this marvel of modern automation. There were no strict visitor regulations. No hair nets, gloves, or special clothing were required to take the tour, only the aforementioned walking shoes. I had no walking shoes, nor do I remember the tour as a quarter-mile. Likely, my father carried me in his arms for most or part of the way. What I do remember, however, is etched forever in my sensory memory.

At the end of the production line, freshly baked loaves of white bread emerged from the oven. There was only white bread, or "light" bread as it is called in Texas—no wheat, whole grain, or designer bread, just white bread—hot, sliced, and ready to be packaged. As we stood there in amazement, the tour guide deftly swept a freshly baked loaf from the conveyor belt. He held it aloft so that all might behold and admire this miracle of modern baking. There was unspoken triumph in the practiced drama of the moment.

And there was an unexpected reward for our attention and interest. He took the loaf of hot bread, separated its thick slices, and slathered each with real butter before offering a whole piece to each person in the group. No sample sizes, no sharing of the bounty. I remember the sheer delight of having a whole piece of hot bread to eat. One fresh from the oven, paired with the simple yet divine taste of butter. As part of the post-war generation, we used oleomargarine at home. It was no substitute at all for the fat pleasure of real butter. The entire experience was wonder and pure joy for a five-year-old child.

During the second half of the twentieth century, the company prospered. The entire community knew exactly when bread was in the oven at the bakery, its yeasty aroma the perfect balance of tang and sweet. The smell of freshly baked bread is the neighborhood lore of an entire generation.

In 1998, Mrs. Baird's Bread was sold to Grupo Industrial Bimbo, Mexico's largest baker and food company. The decision was made to close the Dallas factory, which over time had become functionally obsolete. The last loaves of bread were baked in 2002. It was the end of an era. The community mourned the loss of the intoxicating aroma that perfumed the air with clockwork regularity every day of the week. We grieved the smell, not the product. The bread was still available most anywhere.

The property was later bought by Southern Methodist University. The site was cleared for future development. Rather than implode the low-rise factory, it was not so much torn down as deconstructed. With its robust steel and concrete construction, this was a labor-intensive process.

Over several weeks, the building was carefully dismantled. Likely, there were serious environmental issues with an old factory. As the wrecking ball pounded the solid walls with unrelenting persistence, structural building materials were assembled slowly into large piles. What seemed like only rubble was carefully sorted into twisted piles of salvageable and recyclable material. Other trash and refuse was unceremoniously hauled away by giant dump trucks, load by load, day after day.

The last vestiges of our neighborhood landmark are gone. The vacant lot is now level, prepared for new construction. The pie-shaped site looks clean and vast, an illusion of sheer perspective. A massive John Deere earthmover and its companion front-end loader sit idle in the middle of the lot. Their silence seems to proclaim, "We're finished. Look what we've done." Only a water standpipe protrudes from the surface, a periscope surveying the horizon in search of the future. Random birds peck through freshly turned soil, feverishly in search of nourishment and new life. A wobbly construction fence ripples and sways around the irregular perimeter, its suggestion the outline of that which will yet be.

This is indeed a metaphor for life. The doors open and life begins. We put on our walking shoes and take the tour. We cherish life's moments when our daily bread is slathered with the fresh, buttery goodness of sustained joy, peace, love, and hope. We live productively, useful and steady until irrevocable change stops our progress and shuts down life as it has been.

For a while we experience destruction—"a time to search and a time to give up" (Ecclesiastes 3:6 NIV).

Slowly we understand the value of deconstruction—"a time to tear down and a time to build" (v. 3)—unbuilding in order to rebuild. We sort through the rubble, "a time to scatter stones and a time to gather them" (v. 5). We reorder that which is salvageable and, at last, remove that which is no longer useful—"a time to keep and a time to throw away" (v. 6). The landscape of our life is changed, yet cleared. Our future waits, glistening on the horizon.

We no longer bake fresh bread. We hunger, rather, for new purpose to fill the human space and place that is our being. We are ready for reconstruction. We rebuild and build again unto life. "There is a time for everything, and a season for every activity under the heavens"(v. 1).

Though grief may linger in some small dimension as a whisper in your heart, when the end of the journey nears, the reward is the certainty of your spiritual growth and enrichment. You best incorporate grief into your life when you understand that it is doing its reconstructive work all along your journey as sorrow is transformed into joy. Spiritual growth and enrichment are the rewards of grief; indeed, you may think of them as the gifts that grief gives to you. We honor the steadfast love and faithfulness of God when we acknowledge with gratitude the life-altering gifts of grief to our life. The unimaginable depth and breadth of God's perspective is at the very soul of your spiritual growth through grief.

In the next pages, you will consider the many ways in which God has shown faithfulness to you on your journey through grief. You will contemplate and perhaps identify with the description used to explain the reconstruction of your life at the end of your grief journey. Finally, you will find encouragement to choose life.

The Faithfulness of God

O LORD, you are my God; I will exalt you
and praise your name, for in perfect faithfulness you have
done marvelous things, things planned long ago.
Isaiah 25:1 NIV

Your love, O LORD, reaches to the heavens,
your faithfulness to the skies.
Psalm 36:5 NIV

Give thanks to him, bless his name.
For the LORD is good; his steadfast love endures forever,
and his faithfulness to all generations.
Psalm 100:4-5 NRSV

On a trip to Washington, D.C., in 2006, I decided to make the most of a three-day visit with some rather ambitious sightseeing. Blessed by unseasonably warm weather for late November, I was able to walk the city to view its imposing monuments. Pausing along the way, I read many carefully worded inscriptions. As if awakening from the coma of grief, I experienced a moment of divine illumination. My eyes and heart opened to these eternal truths about the nature of God:

God is ageless.
God is timeless.
God is unchanging.
God is for all generations.

> *God is from everlasting to everlasting.*
> *God is eternal.*
> *God is faithful.*

> *At the World War II memorial, my hand traced slowly over a bronze relief depicting muddy soldiers fighting in the South Pacific, where my own father served for four years. In that moment of spiritual communion, the power of God's faithfulness, God's presence to all soldiers who have ever served, was very personal. God was in the foxhole with my father as he recited Psalm 23 for strength and courage. At the Vietnam Veterans memorial, I found the name of a childhood friend who died in that war, remembering as though yesterday the heartbreak of his parents at the death of their only son. On that brilliant November day, I grasped the reality that God has been there to comfort all who have ever grieved throughout all the ages of time. God is with all those who now serve. Then and there I began to emerge from the spiritual and emotional isolation of grief. I realized with absolute certainty that God is faithful.*

When you attune your inmost heart, you begin to discern with gratitude every manifestation of God's faithfulness, especially as you grieve.

- God protects you. God watches over you (especially if you live alone—perhaps for the first time in life).
- God directs your worry and anxiety toward peace.
- God is with you through the loneliness of grief.
- God instructs you when you are required to make difficult decisions. You listen for God's wisdom in the quiet of your heart: "I bless the Lord who gives me counsel; in the night also my heart instructs me" (Psalm 16:7 NRSV).
- God blesses you with an extra measure of strength and forbearance. You may ask yourself in amazement, "How did I do that?" or "Did I really accomplish that?"
- God holds you in "the everlasting arms" (Deuteronomy 33:27 NIV).
- God lifts you when you are fallen.
- God strengthens you when you are weak.
- God encourages you when you are in despair.
- God wipes away your tears of sorrow.

> *The eternal God is your refuge*
> *and underneath are the everlasting arms.*
> Deuteronomy 33:27 NIV

When I was a little girl, my beloved father came home every day around 5:30 p.m. His routine was reliable and, on most days, quite predictable. His clockwork regularity endowed the dailiness of my young life with an inestimable sense of stability. The pattern of his life was dependable, a quality I grew to appreciate and cherish as a worthy hallmark of a life well lived.

As the owner of a small, successful construction business, my father rose early to meet the demands of a daylight business during normal working hours. He returned home in the late afternoon for a family dinner and whatever activities the evening might require. Sometimes we played basketball on the driveway. He put up the hoop and net lower than regulation height so that my sister and I could learn his moves. In truth, he was a bit of a showboat. In the summer, he would lay out a badminton court on the lawn behind our house. Family rivalry was fierce and intense. Years later, I aced badminton as a physical education requirement in college thanks to the backyard fun of those hot summer nights.

Each day I waited expectantly for my father to come home, listening for his car to pull into the driveway, anticipating his arrival at any moment. From my earliest recollection, we shared a ritual of homecoming love and joy that has grown in rich meaning with each passing year. As soon as my father emerged from the garage, always beautifully dressed, wearing a hat, and carrying a heavy briefcase in his hand, I would rush to him from the house or my waiting place on the porch and greet him with the breathless daily question: "Daddy, can I fly to you?"

The response was split-second, like so much of life. Assuming the answer would be yes to what was really a rhetorical question, I would extend my arms and then my legs in preparation for a spread-eagle leap into space. In one seamless gesture of joyful anticipation, my father would drop his important-looking briefcase straight to the ground and extend his strong, waiting arms with a grin of sheer delight on his wise, handsome face.

Without hesitation, I jumped. It was not the practiced move of a well-trained athlete but a leap straight out as far as it took my young, gangly body to reach the safety of my father's outstretched arms. For one or two seconds I felt the absolute exhilaration of airborne exuberance. The question of whether I might fall from the air and crash to the hard ground never even occurred to me. I was certain that he would be there, ready and able to catch me at the end of the ritual leap. The moment was one of celebration and reunion for father and child at the close of a day apart. And then one day I grew up. I was too big and too heavy for him to catch. I was too old to fly.

I think now of how the simple act of flying out in faith mirrors God's love of father and child. Every day my father modeled the love of God to me through his large, giving spirit. I learned from him the lessons of dependability and reliability. He taught me the love of a faithful heavenly father with the gift of his own steadfast, unconditional love.

As he aged, my father began showing signs of mental and physical deterioration. It was my turn to be the catcher. He relied on the strength of my arms to hold him and carry him through to the end of his life. He honored me with his trust, offered graciously and with full confidence that I would be there for him until the end. I was. I will forever cherish the life and memory of the man who was my father.

Surely, it is God the Father's greatest delight when we, his children, fly into his arms with unquestioning faith, certain that he is utterly dependable and will never let us fall or let us go. Thanks be to God for an extraordinary relationship with a beloved earthly father. Thanks be to God the Father for his divine love.

God's faithfulness is evident in every aspect of your life.

- God provides for your needs.
- God uses others to minister to you in grief.
- God encourages you through the Holy Spirit.

"Know therefore that the LORD your God is God; he is the faithful God, keeping his covenant of love to a thousand generations of those who love him and keep his commands" (Deuteronomy 7:9 NIV). God is faithful. God is with you as you grieve.

Personal Reflections
How has God's faithfulness been manifested to me?

Have I had a moment of awakening to the reality of God's faithfulness to me, especially through grief?

What personal evidence of God's faithfulness do I recognize and cherish?

Reconstruction

Unless the LORD builds the house,
those who build it labor in vain.
Psalm 127:1 NRSV

A contractor or building design specialist perhaps would agree that it is easier to build a new structure than to remodel an old one. Buildings and homes not updated or modernized to current standards usually decline into functional obsolescence after a period of use.

Construction teems with positive energy. The smell of fresh sawdust suggests the promise of a completed project, sparkling new at the end. Reconstruction honors the existence of something worth salvaging, of remaining life within a structure, regardless of its condition. In grief, that structure is your very life; your task is building anew, constructing again.

Remodeling to accommodate life without your loved one is your daily work of grief. As you move forward, your personal reconstruction project may stimulate both your mind and heart, stretching you to contemplate practically endless possibilities for new life.

The most essential part of any structure is a sound foundation. "The rain came down, the streams rose, and the winds blew and beat against that house; yet it did not fall, because it had its foundation on the rock" (Matthew 7:25 NIV). When your life is deconstructed by death, your structure may seem near total collapse. Tremors of loss and sorrow quake the bedrock of your soul. Yet you stand—

your footing secured by the unshakeable foundation that never fails. You build your life on the rock, which is the faithful, steadfast love of God. "Unless the LORD builds the house, those who build it labor in vain." (Psalm 127:1 NRSV). The sacred ground on which you rebuild cannot be destroyed. It is indestructible.

My father was in the commercial construction business for thirty-five years, the proud owner of a sole proprietorship dedicated to excellence. On a hot July day, I sat in my car and wept openly as I watched a large, impressively destructive bulldozer knock down his former office building in the name of progress. The physical symbol of his labor and investment over a professional lifetime was reduced to a pile of twisted rubble in a matter of minutes, the remains an odd admixture of dusty, unusable material.

Similarly, when your loved one dies, the ordered structure of your lifetime together is razed, destroyed with a single final breath.

After my father died, I found Luke 14:28-30 marked in his Bible, noted in his precise engineer's handwriting as the Estimator's Verse: "For which of you, desiring to build a tower, does not first sit down and count the cost, whether he has enough to complete it? Otherwise, when he has laid a foundation, and is not able to finish, all who see it begin to mock him, saying, 'This man began to build, and was not able to finish'" (ESV).

Throughout the course of grief you may, likewise, stop, sit down, and count the cost of rebuilding your life.

Personal Reflections
Do I want to expend the effort for an unknown future?

Do I have the stamina, discipline, and will to complete personal reconstruction?

Am I influenced by the judgment and opinion of others as I seek to rebuild a new life of my own design?

Do I have the determination to work at my own pace, with completion at some unknown time, sooner or later?

Some basic principles of construction apply also to the rebuilding of your life after grief. They must be followed for the successful completion of your personal reconstruction project:

There is a plan to follow.

For every building project there is a design, whether conventional or free form. There are also construction steps that must occur in sequential order. Of course, as structure takes form, the plan may change. A newspaper reported that a major urban cultural project was changed more than fifty times. Similarly, the structure of your new life may be altered by circumstance—remarriage, infirmity, or death. When that happens, you change the plan, you try again, and you build forward. You reorder your daily life so that it feels like a comfortable emotional home. The goal is to reconfigure your life into a place in which you want to live.

Construction is hard work.

A construction worker is usually covered in dirt at the end of a day's labor. The hard work of construction requires physical strength, aptitude, skill, and commitment to complete the job with skilled proficiency. Likewise, grief is hard work. Because you are unpracticed, the labor of reconstruction may seem emotionally and physically exhausting. Gradually you build, placing one block of experience carefully upon the last. As your self-renewal project takes form and shape, an improved structure emerges from your building materials of grief.

Construction is handwork.

In construction, heavy machinery is used to clear, dig, and hoist. Industry manufactures and prepares materials; labor-saving tools expedite efficiency. But hands guide the power saw, the nail gun, the riveter, the end of the girder; affixing and fastening into place one nail, one bolt, one rivet, one girder at a time. Construction is essentially the handwork of human beings, the life force of creative energy that elevates building from science to art. If this were not so, complex robotics alone might be used to erect otherwise soulless structures.

The hands of a construction laborer show the wear and tear of hard use. Seldom is a good worker without a bruise under the fingernail, a silent badge of handwork. Similarly, in grief you are likely bruised under your emotional exterior. You may wear figurative gloves to protect yourself from contact, commitment, or the inevitable march of progress through your life. As with a physical bruise, the injury of grief usually resolves over time.

At last, you roll up your sleeves and do the hands-on work of rebuilding your structure as personal growth propels your project forward. The work is messy, the work is dirty, but construction is always productive.

Construction requires tools.

In the handwork of reconstruction, you may use symbolic tools to alter the structure of your life: you hammer, unscrew, saw off, pull out, level, and realign. You modify in order to "start fresh" in your recreated life.

Reconstruction is the work of self-nurture.

Honoring your body with proper care ensures that your new structure is physically and emotionally sound. This involves eliminating self-destructive behavior, affirming yourself for who you are, and recognizing the gifts and graces that are yours to offer in service to God and others.

Reconstruction is the work of faith.

When you rebuild, you build on the Rock—you partner with God. Faith is what inspires you to do the hard work of grief, the handwork of reconstruction. "Unless the LORD builds the house, those who build it labor in vain" (Psalm 127:1 NRSV).

Personal Reflections

How do I reconstruct a good and useful life?

How do I reconstitute my daily existence without my loved one?

How do I remodel from within without the luxury of creating an entirely new personal structure?

Choose Life

Now choose life, so that you and your children may live and that you may love the LORD your God, listen to his voice, and hold fast to him. For the LORD is your life.
Deuteronomy 30:19-20 NIV

One day, someday, you find yourself unexpectedly at the end of grief, wavering still between the past and the future. This is the moment when you decide emphatically to choose life. You rejoin life in the fullness for which God created you. You honor the steadfast love and faithfulness of God when you resolve to live the rest of the life that is yours empowered by your own extraordinary gifts of grief.

> *As I sat at the arboretum on a pre-Thanksgiving fall day, the weather changed. The air grew cold, the gray-green water of the lake roiled in confused waves as winter arrived. The earth was still; the noise of the wind overlaid the sound of water gurgling through the fountain. On that day of reawakening, I thanked God yet again for life.*

Because God endows you with the capacity to think and reason, choice is part of your everyday existence and behavior. You choose because you are alive. When, like everyone, you err, God allows you to experience your choices and even the consequences of your own free will.

If you think about it, you make hundreds of mindless choices each day: what to wear, what to do, where to go, whom to see. Many difficult choices seem imperative after the death of your loved one at a time when you are most vulnerable.

Personal Reflections
Where should I live?

Should I explore employment opportunities or changes?

What must I do to survive without my loved one?

What must I do to live today?

What must I decide now?

What decisions can wait?

Choice suggests that there are options, things that you may decide between or among:

You may decide not to choose.

Why must you choose anything? Mental, emotional, and spiritual inertia occurs when grief will not be moved. This choice is for life in an illusory time and space that no longer exists. The assumption of grief is that you are supposed to *do something* to help yourself in order to survive. If you find yourself stuck, not wanting to be helped in or through your grief, it may be time to seek help.

You may choose to do nothing.

Perhaps your existence is defined only by death. Life lived *in memoriam* is dedicated solely to the memory of your deceased loved one. This is a meager life with little future, a choice for dying while you are still alive. This is not how your loved one would want you to live.

You may choose to wait and see.

This is a wise choice until, gradually, your life becomes less about pain and sorrow and more about hope for the future. When you are ready, you will experience the urge to get off the sidelines and reenter life as an active participant. You wait and see, choose and try, and try again until you find a satisfying rhythm of choice.

You may choose to move forward.

The spirit in which you live is a conscious choice. You are in charge of your own emotional destiny. You may choose to live either in chronic misery as the victim of unrelieved sadness turned inward, or in faith, trusting the promise that God has a plan for your future. When you take action, you do something to help yourself: you stretch. When you stretch in grief, you grow toward God.

When you choose to move forward, you plan. You make informed decisions about your estate, your health care, and your final arrangements. But you are not required to make all of tomorrow's choices today.

You may choose a life of selfless service.

"Choose this day whom you will serve .... But as for me and my household, we will serve the LORD" (Joshua 24:15 NRSV).

When the end of your journey through grief nears, it is your responsibility—indeed, your sacred duty of grief—to choose life in love and service to God and others. You choose, you grow, you live, you love, you serve. "Now choose life.... For the LORD is your life" (Deuteronomy 30:19-20 NIV).

Personal Reflections

What experiences of grief are influencing my choices?

Am I choosing life?

How have I stretched in grief to grow spiritually toward God?

8
LIVING BEYOND GRIEF

8
LIVING BEYOND GRIEF

Natalie Sleeth was a congregant at Highland Park United Methodist Church, where Leighton was senior minister for twenty-three years. When her husband became ill, she wrote the now well-loved words of "Hymn of Promise" at his bedside. As Leighton lay dying, I sang some favorite hymns for his comfort and mine. I searched my mind but could not remember all the words to "Hymn of Promise," one of Leighton's favorites. My voice crackled with heartbreak as I affirmed that "in our doubt there is believing" and "in our life, eternity." This hymn of hope and comfort ministered to Leighton, even in death. It was played as part of the prelude at his funeral. I never hear the song or sing it without thinking of the moment when "Hymn of Promise" perfectly described for Leighton and for me the resurrection and victory over death that is our faith: In our death, a resurrection; at the last, a victory.[1]

You encounter grief as a stranger. You experience it, and at last, you understand it. Perhaps now you see clearly where you have been on your journey through it. Now you are certain that there is life beyond grief. You believe that your life will again be good and whole and joy-filled. "Weeping may linger for the night, but joy comes with the morning" (Psalm 30:5 NRSV). When you embrace anew the rich fullness of life, you are restored to beauty, possibility, and wonder.

On the next pages, you will better understand the power of durable love as you begin to live beyond grief. As you near the end of the journey through grief, you affirm that God has a purpose for you while you yet have breath on this earth. You learn that you best honor your loved one when you actively reenter the world to endow others with the gifts of your spirit as the finest expression of living beyond grief.

Durable Love

Love knows no limit to its endurance, no end to its trust, no fading of its hope; it can outlast anything. It is, in fact, the one thing that still stands when all else has fallen.
1 Corinthians 13:7-8 JBP

Love is the one thing that still stands when all else has fallen. We find the spiritual basis for the reality of durable love in the assurance that "God is love" (1 John 4:16 NRSV). If we know that God is love and that God ordains love, then we believe that love can outlast anything. The love for us of our beloved deceased transcends the event of death. This is the absolute power of love.

On Monday, the day before he died, there was a dawning light, an unspoken signal. Leighton knew that his time was short and that he was leaving forever. He knew that he was dying. His last words were spoken with labored breath on the morning of his last full day, the day he slipped away. In a sermon he once said, "I always try to think that the last word a person says probably is the most important word that person has to say."[2] Was this a self-fulfilling personal theology?

For one shining moment his sweet, adoring spirit returned, as though he realized that he had been emotionally absent from our life and from me. It seemed as though he was joyously returning from a long trip, a trip taken without me, returning to my waiting, welcoming embrace. His face was bright with beatific gratitude, perhaps because, at last, I had agreed to let him go. His eyes and spirit shone as he drew me into the depths of his soul and said, "I love you, I love you, I love you, I love you, I love you, I love you, I love you."

He said, "I love you" seven times. Seven is thought to be the "perfect" number in the Bible. Was this conscious symbolism? Were these the most important words he had to say? It was a powerful and prophetic moment, a gift of love, the fruit of his spirit. His last breaths poured into reaffirming his love for me. The last words that ever left his lips were spoken to me. This moment of perfect reunion, of oneness of soul and spirit, is in my heart forever.

What I understand more and more is what a rare gift true love is. So very few ever know a love such as ours. We were blessed beyond our wildest imaginings.

In any relationship, you create a legacy of love that begs to be given away with abandon. Your legacy of love is part of who you are, available to lavish on those you love and on those in need of hope and encouragement. Your love lives on—and on and on—when you invest in others. William Barclay has written, "When we spend ourselves to help those in trouble, in distress, in pain, in sorrow, in affliction, God is using us as the highway by which he sends his help into the lives of his people. To help another person in need is to manifest the glory of God, for it is to show what God is like."[3]

You grow spiritually when you reach out to comfort and help another in grief by giving your love away with compassion and understanding. When you embrace others who are grieving the loss of a loved one, you offer them the wisdom of a profound shared experience. According to American Christian theologian Robert McAfee Brown, "Death by itself may not encourage connections. It may simply drive home more deeply the solitude of loss. But love encourages, and even builds connections, and there is no way to separate love and death."[4] Love never fails; it can outlast anything.

The time and space you shared in a relationship of love with the one who is lost is both sacred and eternal. Because love can outlast anything, the inner sanctum you shared with your loved one will always be part of who you are, whatever the future. No one can take it away and nothing can destroy it. Slowly you realize that nothing is lost or compromised if you release your tenacious emotional grip and relax into the certainty that love is.

If you have lost your husband or wife and decide at some time to remarry and invite another into your life, you add a new place alongside that which belongs forever to the one you have grieved. The truth about love is this: the more there is, the more there is to give away. Love can outlast anything. In *Sonnets from the Portuguese,* Elizabeth Barrett Browning wrote,

> I love thee with the breath,
> Smiles, tears, of all my life!—and, if God choose,
> I shall but love thee better after death.[5]

The love you have known will never die. It is eternal. Death has not taken it away; it has only separated you in body, but not in heart. As you begin to live fully beyond your grief, perhaps you will acknowledge with profound gratitude, as I have, that the grace of God is the very essence of love at work in our life. Love can outlast anything.

Personal Reflections
What do I do with my earthly, mortal love?

How do I care for it?

How do I nurture it?

How do I spend it?

Gifts of Your Spirit—A Lasting Legacy

> *Precious in the sight of the LORD*
> *is the death of his faithful ones.*
> Psalm 116:15 NRSV

In his book *Longing for Enough in a Culture of More,* the Reverend Paul Escamilla describes those whose lives are well-lived as "durable saints." He writes:

Among the varied ways faithfulness has become the fabric of their lives, one quality has been identifiable again and again: . . . a certain adequacy of means that issues forth in abundance for others.

At their passing, these durable saints have signed the air not so much with fanfare as grace. The ledgers of their lives are long in matters of generosity, self-giving, and trust; more measured in the realm of acquisition and possessions; and slimmest of all in regard to recognition and self-promotion. In other words, over a lifetime they seem . . . to have needed little and offered much.[6]

Gifts of your spirit are the lasting legacy you leave behind when you die. They are yours to invest in those you love while you yet live. Your personal legacy is not one of material possession or wealth. According to the apostle Paul, "We brought absolutely nothing with us when we entered the world and we can be sure we shall take absolutely nothing with us when we leave it" (1 Timothy 6:7-8 JBP). No amount of money or property can substitute for gifts of your spirit.

As a businessperson, I would be remiss if I did not offer some thoughts here on the things of this world, which you may think of as your legacy. You may laugh at the thought, but in fact, there are no U-Hauls on the way to heaven. You cannot take the things of this world with you. If you have amassed an estate of things, if your attic and garage are full, or if you have one or more storage units that are full or overflowing, consider the possibility of radically divesting yourself of things—give it away, sell it, donate it, recycle it, or throw it away. If you need to hire someone to do it or to incentivize a family member to do it with you, now is the time to assess your need for the things of this world.

At one point during his illness, Leighton made a valiant effort to do some rehabilitation. When he went to the therapy area, we commented on the conspicuous presence of a Ford sedan used for physical rehabilitation. An inscription indicated that a friend of mine, who was heir to a large automobile dealership, donated it to the facility many years before.

Almost a year later, I read the obituary notice for my friend in the newspaper. It described her passion for medical research and her interest in the disease from which she died. I was reminded of her large personality and vibrant spirit, and I thought about how lives unknowingly intersect.

While we are in the world, we do not know how our lives touch or affect others as we endeavor to support and help those known and unknown to us. We give of ourselves, but we cannot require or demand that others receive. Yet this is how we unknowingly create our lasting legacy.

Stewardship—being a wise manager of all your God-given gifts and re-sources—is a biblical mandate. Managing the things of this world is among your highest and best stewardship endeavors. If power and control are important to you, make dispositions yourself, rather than leaving this task for others to do after you die. In 2 Corinthians 6:2, Paul writes, "Behold, now is the accepted time" (KJV). I like the word *behold*, especially as used here. Think about the fact that when this word occurs in the Bible, it usually precedes the proclamation of some-thing important. *Behold* gets your attention. It makes you sit up and take notice.

The point is that you should have the pleasure of sharing your things now with those you love. Generosity will energize your enjoyment of life beyond grief and life in the present. A well-edited life gives you peace of mind, peace of heart, and peace of soul. Peace reminds us that our lasting legacy is not one of material possessions or personal wealth.

Personal Reflections

Am I realistic about the disposition of the things of this world?

What am I hanging on to that I need to give away?

Am I making provisions for this part of my legacy so that it does not overshadow my lasting spiritual legacy?

Your greatest legacy reflects the spiritual maturity of grief survived and, at last, conquered—

> The Father of glory, may give to you a spirit of wisdom and revelation as you come to know him, so that, with the eyes of your hearts enlightened, you may know what is the hope to which he has called you, what are the riches of his glorious inheritance among the saints, and what is the immeasurable greatness of his power for us who believe. (Ephesians 1:17-19 NRSV)

Throughout the Epistles, Paul persistently promotes the fruit of the Spirit (see Galatians 5:21-23 ESV). The inventory includes:

- love
- joy
- peace
- patience
- kindness
- goodness
- faithfulness
- gentleness
- self-control

Paul says, in summary, "Against such things there is no law" (Galatians 5:23 ESV). The gifts of your spirit—the gifts you leave others after you are gone—are born of the fruit of the Spirit. The two are inextricably linked. These are the spiritual qualities of your life that live on in others long after you die. Nothing can substitute for gifts of your spirit as your living endowment to those you love.

> As servants of God we have commended ourselves in every way: through great endurance...by purity, knowledge, patience, kindness, holiness of spirit, genuine love, truthful speech, and the power of God....We are treated as...poor, yet making many rich; as having nothing, and yet possessing everything. (2 Corinthians 6:4-10 NRSV)

Your endowment to others is the expression of the personal gifts of your spirit. These are the eternal qualities of your life, the durable substance of spirit that lives on after you die.

Consider some of the qualities that form your lasting legacy.

Love

"And the greatest of these is love" (1 Corinthians 13:13 NRSV). If we could give but one gift, the greatest would be love. The writer of Colossians urges us, "And, above everything else, be truly loving, for love is the golden chain of all the virtues" (3:14 JBP). Consider how you see your love reflected in others. It is true that you are not responsible for whether or not the love you give is received. Perhaps you have known of or personally experienced family dysfunction and estrangement. This is usually the result of human free-will choices and decisions.

There are no perfect families. What you can do is determine the way in which you express and give love, regardless of how it may be received. When you love without expectation, you are indeed a durable saint—needing little, offering much.

Personal Reflections

Do I love unconditionally?

Do I love with abandon?

Do I hold back, first calculating the risk for hurt before I give my love?

Do I love conditionally?

Do I love with reservation?

Do I love with prejudice or despite my prejudice?

Do I love with judgment, or freely and without judgment, solely for the sake of love?

How do I react when my love is not received in the spirit in which I have given it?

Goodness

"Surely goodness and mercy shall follow me all the days of my life" (Psalm 23:6 NRSV). A life of authentic goodness inspires and enriches by example. A pure heart and unmixed motives are manifestations of genuine goodness, the lasting legacy of a memorable life. This is how to build a life of authentic goodness:

> His divine power has given us everything we need for life and godliness, through the knowledge of him who called us by his own glory and goodness.... For this very reason, you must make every effort to support your faith with goodness, and goodness with knowledge, and knowledge with self-control, and self-control with endurance, and endurance with godliness, and godliness with mutual affection, and mutual affection with love. (2 Peter 1:3-7 NRSV)

These are the steps, beginning with faith and ending with love. This is the biblical standard for authentic goodness.

Personal Reflections
What is authentic goodness?

Do I know someone who is an authentically good person?

What qualities describe a life of authentic goodness?

Service

"Serve one another in love" (Galatians 5:13 NIV). A heart of service thrives in perpetuity. Imperceptibly you contribute to the formation of others as you model selfless servant leadership. When you "serve one another in love," you give the gift of yourself. Joan Wester Anderson writes,

> We can all be angels to one another. We can choose to obey the still small stirring within, the little whisper that says "Go. Ask. Reach out. Be an answer to someone's plea. You have a part to play. Have faith." We can decide to risk that He is indeed there, watching, caring, cherishing us as we love and accept love.
> The world will be a better place for it.
> And wherever they are, the angels will dance.[7]

A few months after Leighton died, I dared to think about reclaiming our master bedroom. Could I sleep again in the bed in which he lay so sick before he went to the hospital where he died? Intuitively I knew that to find the courage to venture back to our marriage bed, it would take at least a new mattress. Could I spend the money? The sheets should be replaced, but the expense seemed out of the question. I could afford to do both, but I did not think so at the time.

I was not completely committed to moving back into our room, yet I decided to try. It could be too painful. I hesitated. On an autumn Saturday when the rest of the world seemed at play, I went to the mattress store, hoping to take delivery that day. It must be that day. It seemed a "now or never" proposition.

The owner, who over time had sold us several mattresses, said that he would have to get one from the warehouse, which would take two days. I was ready to abandon the idea, not sure I could ever sleep in our bed again. Would I forever after ignore the room and bed as I passed through on the way to my closet and bathroom? The delay seemed a good enough excuse to capitulate.

The doorbell rang around 5:30 p.m. It was the storeowner, standing there with a new mattress top. His response to my need was not about making a sale or even customer service. He had seen my distress and had compassion. On me. This act of human kindness meant more than any other expression of comfort. He saw my grief, sensed my urgency, and did something about it. He was late to a birthday party because he selflessly took the time to go to the warehouse and make a personal delivery. He was an angel, a very real one, as he ministered that day to me.

Faith

You give the gift of faith and teach your faith by example. Those you love learn best about your faith by how you live. Your spiritual estate is character and integrity, formed by the discipline of faith. "I know, my God, that you test the heart and are pleased with integrity" (1 Chronicles 29:17 NIV). God tests your heart and is pleased with integrity. Consider your spiritual estate as the measure of a life well lived in faith.

Personal Reflections
Who am I in my inmost heart?

What are the qualities of my soul?

How would I describe myself?

What three words would I use to characterize who I am?

Do I think that others would use the same words?

Do I believe in one way yet live in another?

Compassion

You are a benefactor of compassion when you reach out with a heart fortified from within by your experience of grief. You best teach compassion to those you love by your spiritual reaction to life's trials and tragedies. When from sorrow you learn the hard-won lessons of humanity and compassion, then you are able to join hands with others and communicate heart to heart, "I hurt with you, I share your pain, and I love you." Yours is then the heart and voice of emotional and spiritual authenticity. Your gift of compassion to others is never forgotten. There is perhaps no finer gift of your spirit than to endow those you love with a sensibility for compassion.

Hope

As you look ahead, eager to move forward, you discern at last that for which you should hope. You endow those you love with the glory of hope when, by example, you live with expectancy, patience, and trust.

It would indeed be your worthiest epitaph if you live as a durable saint and one day die to your glorious inheritance in the saints, knowing that you created a lasting legacy by giving the gifts of your eternal spirit to those you love.

Personal Reflections

What are my qualities that I see reflected in those I love?

What words would I use to describe my best qualities, those I would like to endow?

What words would I use to describe the qualities I would not like to see reflected in others?

Beyond my family, where do I see a reflection of my investment in others or in institutions?

Where have I planted the seeds that will become my lasting legacy?

What words describe how I would like others to remember me?

What would I want to be said of me at my funeral or memorial/celebration of life service?

Dr. Margaret Farley, Professor of Christian Ethics at Yale Divinity School, states this about faith:

> Faith leads us, it is true, through valleys of darkness and into the shadow of death. But all the while, it leads into life, and it knows the ways not only of sadness, but of joy. By it we are carried into God's own life; in it we can find one another; through it we come home even to ourselves. Incredible work, radical surrender, unlimited future, inexhaustible life—these are not illusions only if it is true that "Nothing is impossible with God." If these are not illusions, then they do bear pondering, even as aspects of the concept of faith—believing, believing in and believing into the God who has been revealed in Jesus Christ.[8]

On the last occasion that my beloved husband was in the pulpit, he offered this pastoral prayer, a benediction to our grief journey: "We have come this far by faith, and we will continue to walk with our hand in yours wherever you lead us." Pain and sorrow are vanquished by faith; death is rendered powerless as you at last traverse the valley of the shadow of death and grief is no more. Death does not leave you ambivalent in your resolve to claim new life at the end of your journey through grief. Thanks be to God for the victory over death.

SUPPLEMENT

9

GRIEF AT THE HOLIDAYS

9
GRIEF AT THE HOLIDAYS

Just because I was grieving, I was not required to block the festivities of the holiday from my life; I was allowed to participate. And so I mixed it up with the crowds and noise, watching and listening for sights and sounds as I moved in my spirit toward Emmanuel. I heard a solo trombone on the sidewalk offering "O Come, O Come, Emmanuel." My thoughts began to awaken.

I waited for a cab and heard "Angels We Have Heard on High." My mind stirred; I remembered that this is my favorite Christmas carol.

At church, the message of awakening seeped through my spiritual consciousness as the smell of incense assaulted my senses with its symbolism of prayer and joy and hope. The lights on Park Avenue shouted, "It's not too late; don't miss it!" So I allowed my pragmatic resistance to all things commercial to thaw a bit, humbled by the man on the street with only one foot, silently asking for alms, his spirit surprised and grateful when I honored his entreaty. His dog was with him, perhaps to give him warmth, perhaps to help him as a faithful companion. He had a friend; he was less alone than I was.

The man who slept in a doorway at the church was not there, yet his neatly packed worldly possessions stood on the sidewalk in

> *testimony to his very existence. I tucked a bill into his bundle. It was my Christmas joy to provide even a small token in acknowledgment of his life. Perhaps as he unrolled his bed in search of warmth and protection from another freezing night he would find it and know that someone cares. Emmanuel, God with us. I was on the way to the manger, the experience of Christmas.*

Your journey through grief is marked by inevitable secular and sacred holidays. Even under the best circumstances, holidays are emotion-laden occasions. With the rapid succession of Thanksgiving, Christmas, and the New Year, November and December can be painful, prolonged days of remembrance. When you grieve at the holidays, you agonize about what is to come because of the unknown—that is, how things will be rather than how things have been. Likely, you live in the shadow of expectation; you may cherish both high hopes and dismal fears. Most often your reality is somewhere in between.

Probably you have experienced an instinctive sense of aversion when print advertising and television commercials assault you prematurely with stealth campaigns that draw your attention inevitably to the extended holiday season. It seems that advertising and decorating begin earlier each year. You are inescapably hostage to rampant commercialism. You may groan, but at some point you slowly succumb to its insistence, as we all do.

You may be among the many people who dread the holidays because of the unavoidable pressure to do, buy, and experience, urged upon you during the season. The nature of grief is that it intensifies your experience of occasions that painfully remind you of your loss. Dread may creep into your heart as you begin to imagine what the holiday season will be like. You may ask, "How can there be celebration without the one I love?"

It is normal to be fearful when you are grieving, especially as you anticipate or even dread the holiday season. *Dread* is "fearful or distasteful anticipation"[1] that may express itself as disquiet, worry, or distress, some of the familiar emotions of grief. Dread is, in fact, the extreme form of fear.

> *Be strong and of good courage, do not fear or be in dread…for it is the LORD your God who goes with you; he will not fail you or forsake you.*
> Deuteronomy 31:6 RSV

To understand dread at the holidays, you must simultaneously acknowledge and deconstruct your fear. Remember that fear is a basic human response, especially when you are grieving. As you approach the season, remember that *your anticipation is usually much worse than the actual holiday.* Often you resolve much of your fear ahead of time and the day is not as difficult as you expected.

> For I, the LORD your God,
> hold your right hand;
> it is I who say to you, "Do not fear,
> I will help you."
> Isaiah 41:13 NRSV

In the following pages, you will discover some specific coping strategies for managing your grief at the holiday season. Next, you will consider the difference between the festival of Christmas and the experience of Christmas. Finally, you will be guided in your search for the light of Christmas amid your grief.

The Season

I will be with you; I will not fail you or forsake you.
Joshua 1:5 NRSV

If this is the first holiday season without your loved one, a tidal wave of emotion may engulf you. When you grieve at the holidays, your heart is attuned to the sadness of loss and pain. If you are tearful or depressed, your heartfelt tears may cue your family members to express their emotions as well. Worry about crying is a hardship of grief compounded by the holidays. When you release your tears, you experience physical and emotional relief, a welcome catharsis to your grief.

As you grieve at this affective time of the year, these strategies may help you through the season:

Put the day in perspective.

The actual holiday is just one day, twenty-four hours. For weeks on end, life is pressured by commercial, social, and spiritual suggestions that demand a larger-than-life experience of the holidays. Inflamed by the secular world, intense emotions overlay grief for what seems an interminable holiday season. The holiday itself is just one day. Put the day in perspective.

Know your limits.

Be intentional about the extent to which you participate—how little or how much you want to do. You are the only person in charge of you; be in touch with yourself. If a situation is too difficult, limit your exposure or choose not to take part. It is easy to be swept along by the good intentions of family and friends who want to distract you from your pain. If you are pressured to do too much, you may instinctively retreat. Know your limits and resolve not to exceed them. The word most seldom used at the holidays is no. You may say no; do not be afraid to say no. Just say no.

Plan.

Before the death of your loved one, there was probably always a plan. If this is the first holiday without the one you grieve, make a plan and structure the holidays accordingly. Be timely in making airline or hotel reservations; communicate your plan to family. Whether your plan succeeds or is not quite what you expected, a plan for the holidays precludes the emotional hangover of discouragement and frustration if you have made no plan at all. Make a plan. Have a plan.

Take care of yourself.
- Get enough rest. The holidays are draining: physically, emotionally, mentally, and spiritually.
- Consider having a "good enough" holiday, rather than a perfect holiday. Do not set expectations too high for yourself or the day. Before the death of your loved one, there were probably some disappointing holiday seasons.
- Think about how to make it through just *this* holiday. There will be other holidays.
- Live one day at a time; stay in the moment.
- Turn off the television and limit trips to retail environments to manage the daily, artificial urgency of the commercial holiday season.
- Guard your heart. The holidays are the most stressful time of the year. Do not trivialize or discount the real physical stress caused by grief. If you manifest any heart-related symptoms or signs of stress, seek immediate treatment.
- Take time for yourself on holidays—time to reflect, time to remember, time to forget.
- Let others know that they are not responsible for making you happy. Even if your loved one would "want you to be happy," you do not have to be happy. Being happy, however, is not a betrayal of your loved one. When,

one day, life returns more to happiness, holidays will be easier to manage. The experience of most is that, eventually, they do enjoy the holidays again.

- With life going on all around you at the holidays, seemingly at full tilt, make an extra effort to forgive those comforters who try to console you with empty words or gestures. Likely, you expect others to understand what you are feeling at this time of the year, but it is not possible. You alone know the depth of your grief, especially at the holidays.

Personal Reflections

Do I have trouble sleeping?

Do I overeat or have no appetite?

Do I worry constantly?

Do I have increased heart rate or rapid breathing while at rest?

Am I irritable, angry, or impatient?

Am I tired?

Am I unable to concentrate?

What is a "good enough" holiday for me?

Am I guarding my heart?

Am I taking time for myself?

If you are experiencing any constellation of these grief-related stress symptoms at the holidays, it is important to seek the help of a physician or trained professional for adequate and proper care.

Decide about traditions.

Holidays usually center on tradition. When fractured by death, you may decide to continue family traditions, or you may want to create new traditions that honor the memory of your loved one. What you do this year does not have to become a permanent tradition. Your experience of grief may change the way you approach the holidays; you may decide on a new format for the future.

Be realistic about family.

At the holidays, you want the "picture" to remain the same. That is, you would like to continue envisioning your family as it was before the death of your loved one. Many seasonal illustrations by Norman Rockwell idealize the family as a multigenerational group, clearly connected by warmth and love. Perhaps these familiar images convince you that family life should resemble the ideal. Contemporary experience affirms that art does not imitate life. Divorce, blended families, dysfunctional relationships, addictions, and ordinary bad behavior are the realities that belie the ideal of an intact nuclear family gathered together in peace to share a loving, joyful holiday celebration.

Though holidays mean "family together," gatherings may be difficult. Your family may want everything "back to normal." You may experience subtle pressure to be appropriately cheerful and gay; you may be expected to "be over it." Grief makes it difficult to participate fully in festivities. It seems that your family is trying to forget what you most want to remember.

Acting as if no one died denies grief at the very moment when the comfort of family is most needed. Be proactive and decide together about the holidays. Communicate and be sensitive to one another. Remember that there is no right or wrong way to experience the holidays, the season, or the actual twenty-four-hour day. So . . .

- Realize that it is not going to be easy.
- Do the things that are special or important to you.
- Do the best that you can.

God knows your heart as you grieve at the holidays. Receive God's promise: "I will be with you, I will not fail you or forsake you" (Joshua 1:5 NRSV).

Personal Reflections
What am I dreading about the holiday season?

What is the reality of the "picture" this year?

Why am I afraid of the reality?

The Experience

To you is born this day in the city of David a Savior,
who is the Messiah, the Lord.
Luke 2:11 NRSV

Christmas may evoke memories that trigger and sustain your grief. The contrast between sorrow and celebration is almost unbearable because many of your best memories are perhaps in the context of holiday celebrations. You may be painfully aware of the absence of your loved one, who likely was among the most important people in your interpersonal sphere. Poet Edna St. Vincent Millay wrote, "The presence of that absence is everywhere."[2] You endow Christmas with emotional power as you remember the past with intense yearning for the one whose presence brought joy to your life.

Many people celebrate Christmas in two ways:

- the festival of Christmas
- the experience of Christmas

The festival of Christmas celebrates the season and the day. Likely, your secular reference is tradition, now skewed by grief. As you gather with family, or others you choose as family, you realize that the festival of Christmas will never be the same again without your loved one. In 1928, Umphrey Lee, president of Southern Methodist University from 1939 to1954, greeted the congregation of Highland Park United Methodist Church with these seasonal thoughts:

As we grow older, watching the passing of plans and men, feeling the touch of winter upon our heads and upon our hearts, we come to look forward to Christmas as the Festival of Beginning Again. The eternal youth of Christianity is in its insistence upon life, not upon life as mere duration here or hereafter, but upon that surging vitality of soul and spirit which is renewed hope, recovered love, belief in the future. All this the Christian means when he testifies: "I believe in God." The essential faith begins with Bethlehem and the Child. He is forever that symbol of new life which is reborn in men today, a life that will not be bound by prejudice or meanness, that will not be held by our weakness nor by the gates of Death.

May you all be happy at this Festival of Beginning Again.[3]

Personal Reflections

Is it too much effort to put up a tree?

Will I decorate, or should the ornaments stay packed away this year?

Is it too painful for me to send Christmas cards?

Is gift selection a daunting task without the concurrence of my loved one?

Within the festival, your heart seeks the deeper experience of Christmas. Sometimes it happens; sometimes it does not. For a while, your joy in the world may seem a remembrance from a life passed away. But Christmas may come to you in small, private moments when your heart is strangely touched by joy. The experience of Christmas may surprise you with the mystery of comfort. Amid the chaos of grief, the moment of Christmas may take your breath away with its life-renewing peace.

Grief is an opportunity to discover anew the true meaning of Christmas—God's love for humankind. Christmas happens when your heart discerns divine love indwelling. This is the love that holds you close in grief. This is the love that restores you and makes you whole again. Emmanuel, God with us . . .

- to comfort you
- to redeem you
- to restore you
- to give you peace
- to hold you in the communion of saints with the one you have loved and lost

Look for a sign; it will overwhelm you as the certainty of life beyond death reaches into your heart with the unmistakable gift of God's love. The experience of Christmas may come to you any day, not just on December 25. Expect it; look for it; be open to it. Christmas comes when someone reaches out to you in love. Christmas comes when you reach out to someone in love. Expect an unexpected blessing; be a blessing to others. Christmas. Emmanuel. God with us.

I am your friend and my love for you goes deep.

There is nothing I can give you which you have not got, but there is much, very much, that, while I cannot give it, you can take.

No heaven can come to us unless our hearts find rest in today. Take heaven!

No peace lies in the future which is not hidden in this present little instant. Take peace!

The gloom of the world is but a shadow. Behind it, yet within our reach is joy.

There is a radiance and glory in the darkness could we but see— and to see we have only to look. I beseech you to look!

Life is so generous a giver, but we, judging its gifts by the covering, cast them away as ugly, or heavy or hard. Remove the covering and you will find beneath it a living splendor, woven of love, by wisdom, with power.

Welcome it, grasp it, touch the angel's hand that brings it to you. Everything we call a trial, a sorrow, or a duty, believe me, that angel's hand is there, the gift is there, and the wonder of an overshadowing presence. Our joys, too, be not content with them as joys. They, too, conceal diviner gifts.

Life is so full of meaning and purpose, so full of beauty—beneath its covering—that you will find earth but cloaks your heaven.

Courage, then, to claim it, that is all. But courage you have, and the knowledge that we are all pilgrims together, wending through unknown country, home.

And so, at this time, I greet you. Not quite as the world sends greetings, but with profound esteem and with the prayer that for you now and forever, the day breaks, and the shadows flee away.

Fra Giovanni Giocondo (1433-1513)[4]

The Light

The people who walked in darkness
Have seen a great light;
Those who dwelt in the land of the shadow of death,
Upon them a light has shined.
Isaiah 9:2 NKJV

Christmas lights symbolize the festival. Each one is a brilliant celebration of life. The reality of grief is that the death of your loved one has darkened your life. At Christmas, darkness seeks the light and becomes the light: "The people who walked in darkness have seen a great light; those who dwelt in the land of the shadow of death, upon them a light has shined" (Isaiah 9:2 NKJV). This is the light that shines out of your darkness with the promise that there is yet life beyond grief. Christmas is about the light of the world, God's love illuminating your darkness.

The words of "A Hymn for Advent" are powerful and evocative: "God says: Light! And makes our day; fear and chaos lose their say."[5] At Christmas, chaos may roil your emotions. There may be chaos in your family or home. The clamor of the secular world may incite chaos in your heart. But light overwhelms and defeats chaos. Light is the reason for Christmas, the light of God's love, Emmanuel, God with us.

There are many incarnations of light—candlelight, incandescent light, sunlight, moonlight, the radiance of brilliant stars. The psalmist declares, "In your light we see light" (Psalm 36:9 NRSV). In grief, light is in the delicate balance between your sadness and your hope for the future. Light is in your heightened peace as you move toward acceptance. Light is in your enjoyment of one or two aspects of the holiday season and in surviving largely intact. Light is in your understanding of the gift—joy. Indeed, "Light dawns for the righteous, and joy for the upright in heart" (Psalm 97:11 NRSV).

You have the power to direct your grief as you direct the light. When you block the light and, instead, choose darkness, you become a holiday victim, for in darkness there is no light. Finding the light means managing the darkness. Unlike gradations of light, dark is dark; darkness is darkness. "If then the light in you is darkness, how great is that darkness!" (Matthew 6:23 NRSV). If you dwell in darkness, overwhelmed by negative emotions and immobilized by grief, ask for help. Let another guide you back into the light.

Grief may seem like an eternal night, as if your light is overcome for a while by darkness. Slowly, with divine radiance, receding darkness yields to dawn. The rosy aura of sunrise bathes the softness of morning with the light of reawakening life. As love and hope creep imperceptibly onto the horizon, you greet the new day of the rest of your life with expectation and tentative joy—your soul again enlivened by the warmth of light. *See the light.*

Just as there is no one experience of loss, so also there is no one experience of light. Light shines in quiet meditation. Light shines in moments of prayer and thanksgiving. It shines when you light a candle to honor the memory of your loved one. Remember that your shared light shines forever. Love is the divine link to the eternal spiritual presence of the one you have loved and lost. As you create light and discover your light within, each day holds the promise of remembrance, release, and expression. *Walk in the light.*

Christmas is the celebration of light. Receive the blessing when moments of light shine in your heart. Be at peace in the certainty that death is not the end. *Seek the light.*

Personal Reflections

How am I seeking the light at Christmas?

What manifestations of light minister to me as I grieve at Christmas?

Do I dwell in darkness, resisting the light?

How do I direct the light to shine into my grief?

10
PEACE OF MIND:
FINANCIAL MANAGEMENT FOR LIFE

).

10
PEACE OF MIND:
FINANCIAL MANAGEMENT FOR LIFE

Following a second surgery over the long Memorial Day weekend, I sat in the waiting area outside the intensive care unit, between visits to Leighton's bedside. I was allowed into the ICU for a few minutes every hour. Sensing a race against time, I worked feverishly trying to incorporate his manual bookkeeping system into my computer program. In quiet desperation, my inner voice urged, "Be productive; make use of the time."

With trepidation, I realized that I was now in charge of our joint personal business. I was suddenly responsible for our financial management after eighteen years of separate accounts and disparate bookkeeping methods. Leighton was an organized, efficient manager who preferred a number two pencil, a red bookkeeping pencil, and a ledger page for accounting. I prefer computers and technology. It stretched my mind and emotions to learn his system and to incorporate, almost against my will, another new mode of thinking and doing into a life already awash in chaos.

I felt particularly unsure about managing our health insurance. This was his responsibility. Anxiety intensified self-doubt as my fear grew daily over the probable death of my husband. It was unimaginable that he would not be there to administer our life.

On one visit to the ICU, he was remarkably lucid. Perhaps sensing my uncertainty, he wanted to talk about our business, a mercifully neutral, nonmedical subject in which we were both interested. Among other things, we had received our annual renewal statement for membership to the Dallas Arboretum. My impulse was to cancel it. He said with assurance and an implied confidence in the future, "Oh, no, renew the Arboretum." He could not know that this would become my place of retreat and solace "beside the still water." For many months after his death, I went there to journal and grieve.

I asked Leighton about paying some of the medical bills. The statements were arriving almost daily in the mail. Each ominous envelope struck fear in my heart. He was certain that the deductible had been satisfied and advised that I should wait for the claims to work through the system. I was overwhelmingly grateful for his wise counsel and this brief momentary return of his strong leadership. His unemotional confidence in business management strengthened me that day.

A few weeks after Leighton died, I was working at my office, trying to make order out of our personal business. My profession is family business management. Although I have been in business for over thirty years, I was painfully aware of feeling anxious, fearful, unsure, and lacking in self-confidence. That was not at all like me. I was overwhelmed by my sense of total vulnerability. It occurred to me that if I were feeling this way after doing business as a professional for many years, what must others—who have limited financial management experience—feel when death occurs and they are similarly overwhelmed by grief?

In the weeks and months that followed, my need for closure on the business of his illness and death was visceral. Every envelope and piece of paper that was a medical bill or statement ripped open the wound of my heart again and again and again. It took over ten months to settle the bills and insurance claims. It was an agonizing process, made bearable only by the patient, persistent intervention of our insurance advocate. She was an angel who became my friend.

With her support, I protested the last disputed medical bill, a large hospital claim that had been denied. My impulse was to pay and be finished, but I knew that I did not owe the money. I knew, too, that Leighton would expect me to be tough and hold out, a primal test of fortitude in a life already so broken. In the end, I prevailed, claiming a major moral and financial victory over the unwieldy institutional bureaucracy that marches dispassionately through our lives.

On the next pages, you will be introduced to an easy system designed to help you take charge of the financial management of your life. Included are some forms with information that everyone, especially those who grieve, should assemble and have available. Finally, there is an action plan of things to consider for your life, especially if you live alone.

Personal Business Management

For God has not given us a spirit of fear, but of power and of love and of a sound mind.
2 Timothy 1:7 NKJV

Financial management can be a daunting challenge for anyone at any time of life. It is especially important with advancing age, in the event of illness, or at the death of a loved one. When you grieve, life may seem out of control on many levels. Perhaps, as I did, you exist for a while in a dense fog, your best judgment impaired by unfamiliar mental chaos, distraction, and confusion. You may lack information and understanding, which is often a cause of anxiety and helplessness. Personal business and financial management can easily overwhelm you, especially at the time of grief.

After Leighton's death, I spent several months struggling to make order out of our personal business. Because of my experience with financial management through grief, I prepared the information in this chapter to assist others with the management of their businesses after the death of a loved one. You may feel barely adequate to the task of financial management, but there is no standard; where you are is good enough. *Not knowing* causes fear, which is part of every crisis in life. The information provided here is very basic. It is not about creating or amassing wealth. It is about empowering you to manage successfully what you have. The desired goals are:

1. RELIEF FROM CHAOS through simplified financial understanding and management.

2. REASSURANCE and ENCOURAGEMENT that anyone can manage and master finances.

3. PEACE in the continuity of life, especially during advancing age, illness, and grief.

The fact is that *no one cares about your money as much as you care about your money*. Even trusted advisors, children, and those who provide financial services and offer you well-meant advice and recommendations, are not personally invested in your financial health and well-being. When possible, no one should rely entirely on others for important financial management decisions unless he or she is physically or mentally unable to function or cope.

Several factors may influence your emotions about finances and money:

- Money attitudes learned from others
  - how your parents communicated about money
  - how you communicated with your spouse about money
  - your own self-confidence in personal money management

- Your actual financial condition
  - your realistic understanding of your assets and liabilities
  - your commitment to living within your means

Managing money positively and proactively may benefit your changed life in:

- Empowerment—having control over that which is quantifiable (money)
- Peace of mind—learning hands-on management (finance and business)
  - you understand what resources are available for your use (income)
  - you take charge of your day-to-day personal business administration (budgeting)
- Financial independence

Money management is business. It does not merit an investment of the precious emotional energy that must be directed to issues of your heart, mind, and spirit when you grieve. Though you may feel inadequate to the task of your own financial management, remember this important point that bears repeating: *no one cares about your money as much as you care about your money*. The following information is a guide for the preparation of a comprehensive, permanent record of personal and business information for your own reference and for those who assist you or who will settle your estate. Consider this part of your lasting legacy. The discipline of financial management enables you to meet both opportunity and adversity with peace of mind.

There are four essential steps for effective financial management:

- ASSESSMENT
- ORGANIZATION
- INVENTORY
- ANALYSIS

As you move through these steps, there are five basic objectives:

1. Simplify.
2. Create a permanent record.
3. Develop a system of organization.
4. Create an accurate and comprehensive financial inventory.
5. Create a workable budget.

Remember that the information you will assemble is a work in progress. Schedule an appointment with yourself and your advisors (personal or professional) to review and update your information at least once a year. The goal is to create a workable system of financial management for your life going forward.

Step 1: Assessment

Start now. Start where you are. Start with what you have. Begin with the everyday tasks.

- Assemble the checkbooks. Determine how much money is available in the accounts on which you are authorized to sign. Could you close or consolidate some accounts? Objectively assess your need for multiple bank accounts.
- Assemble the bills that must be paid. Pay these on time. Consider setting up automatic payments from a checking account for utility bills, mortgage payments, car payments, and monthly insurance premiums.

- Arrange for direct deposit of social security, pension, and paychecks into a designated account, which eliminates trips to the bank for deposit.
- Assemble files that are familiar and readily accessible.
- Make a general list—a preliminary overview—of your assets as you understand them.

The objective of ASSESSMENT is to take care of the business that requires your immediate attention and generate a preliminary overview of your personal finances.

Step 2: Organization

Begin to assemble as much specific information as possible for your permanent record.

- Devise a filing system that is logical and workable for you. What is efficient for one person may be difficult, inconvenient, or complicated for another.
- Have a shredder available to dispose of personal information, records, and files that are out of date or no longer needed.
- Develop the habit of shredding mail (junk, solicitations, etc.) for your protection against identity theft and fraud.
- Register your telephone numbers with do-not-call lists as an additional privacy safeguard.

If the person in your life who has been responsible for earning, providing, and managing is incapacitated or dies, it is important for you to take legal and emotional ownership of your assets.

The objective of ORGANIZATION is to create order for you and build a system for your efficient financial management.

Step 3: Inventory

Begin to make an inventory of your assets and liabilities.

- Assemble information
  - Real Estate/Real Property

- Property Insurance
- Credit Card Accounts

- Using the forms on pages 194–95, prepare a statement of your
  - Assets
  - Liabilities
  - Income

The objective of INVENTORY is to create a comprehensive, detailed record of your assets, liabilities, and income.

Step 4: Analysis

Complete a comprehensive financial assessment using the forms on pages 00-00. Use the assembled information for:

- Your Personal Financial Inventory (page 196)
- Your Personal Monthly Management Budget (pages 197–98)

The objective of ANALYSIS is for you to understand your assets and liabilities. This provides a clear picture for you of the standard of living you can reasonably expect and comfortably afford.

Ongoing financial management—using the steps of assessment, organization, inventory, and analysis—is peace of mind that builds for the future. Your stewardship will honor your loved one for generations to come.

Use the forms and worksheets on the following pages to help create an overview of your personal business. You may copy these pages to begin and later update your management system as changes occur.

Overview of Assets, Liabilities, Income

ASSETS

1. BANK ACCOUNTS
NAME OF ACCOUNT HOLDER(S)_____

NAME OF INSTITUTION_____

ACCOUNT NUMBER/STYLE   **SIGNATORIES**

CHECKING_____

      APPROXIMATE BALANCE_____

MONEY MARKET SAVINGS_____

      APPROXIMATE BALANCE_____

CERTIFICATE OF DEPOSIT_____

      FACE VALUE_____

      INTEREST RATE_____

      MATURITY DATE_____

      INTEREST_____

2. BROKERAGE ACCOUNTS
NAME OF ACCOUNT HOLDER_____

NAME OF INSTITUTION_____

SECURITIES HELD   **SHARES**   **APPROXIMATE VALUE**

STOCKS_____

_____

BONDS_____

_____

MUTUAL FUNDS_____

_____

MONEY MARKET ACCOUNT(S)_____

_____

3. MUTUAL FUND/INDIVIDUAL STOCK ACCOUNTS
NAME OF FUND/STOCK

      NUMBER OF SHARES HELD/FUND BALANCE_____

      NAME OF ACCOUNT HOLDER_____

      PARTICIPANT NUMBER_____

      NAME OF INSTITUTION_____

LIABILITIES

MORTGAGE LOANS:

      HOMESTEAD_____ $_____

      SECOND HOME_____ $_____

      RENTAL PROPERTIES_____ $_____

      HOME EQUITY LOAN_____ $_____

AUTOMOBILE LOANS/LEASES_____ $_____

CREDIT CARD DEBT_____ $_____

NOTES PAYABLE_____ $_____

LOANS FROM BROKERAGE MARGIN ACCOUNT_____ $_____

BANK LOANS _____ $_____

UNPAID/DEFERRED IRS TAX LIABILITY_____ $_____

ESTIMATE OF TOTAL LIABILITIES _____ $_____

NET WORTH = ASSETS MINUS LIABILITIES _____ $_____

ESTIMATE OF NET WORTH _____ $_____

INCOME

SALARY AND BONUSES_____ $_____

DEFERRED COMPENSATION_____ $_____

SOCIAL SECURITY_____ $_____

PENSION PLAN_____ $_____

INVESTMENT INCOME_____ $_____

IRA_____ $_____

ALIMONY_____ $_____

CHILD SUPPORT_____ $_____

ESTIMATE OF TOTAL INCOME PER YEAR _____ $_____

ESTIMATE OF INCOME TAXES OWED PER YEAR _____ $_____

ESTIMATE OF NET INCOME PER YEAR _____ $_____

ESTIMATE OF TOTAL INCOME PER MONTH _____ $_____

PERSONAL FINANCIAL INVENTORY

ASSETS

CHECKING ACCOUNT(S) _____ $_____

SAVINGS ACCOUNT(S)_____ $_____

CERTIFICATES OF DEPOSIT_____ $_____

MONEY MARKET FUNDS_____ $_____

INVESTMENTS:

      STOCKS _____ $_____

      BONDS_____ $_____

      MUTUAL FUNDS_____ $_____

      IRA_____ $_____

ANNUITIES_____ $_____

LIFE INSURANCE AND DEATH BENEFITS_____ $_____

COMPANY BENEFITS:

      STOCK OPTIONS_____ $_____

      SAVINGS/401(k) PLANS_____ $_____

      ESOP/PAYSOP_____ $_____

      PENSION PLAN_____ $_____

      DEFERRED COMPENSATION_____ $_____

REAL ESTATE:

      HOMESTEAD_____ $_____

      SECOND HOME_____ $_____

      RENTAL PROPERTIES_____ $_____

      MORTGAGES/DEEDS RECEIVABLE_____$_____

REAL PROPERTY:

      OIL AND GAS INTERESTS_____ $_____

      PARTNERSHIP INTERESTS_____ $_____

PERSONAL PROPERTY:

      FINE ART_____ $_____

      JEWELRY_____ $_____

      HOUSEHOLD FURNISHINGS _____ $_____

      AUTOMOBILES_____ $_____

      OTHER PERSONAL EFFECTS_____ $_____

ESTIMATE OF TOTAL ASSETS_____ $_____

PERSONAL MONTHLY MANAGEMENT BUDGET

GROSS INCOME

SALARY/WAGES/COMPENSATION_____ $_____

SOCIAL SECURITY_____ $_____

IRA_____ $_____

ANNUITY_____ $_____

PENSION PLAN_____ $_____

INVESTMENT INCOME_____ $_____

ESTIMATE OF TOTAL GROSS MONTHLY INCOME_____ $_____

ESTIMATE OF TOTAL GROSS ANNUAL INCOME_____ $_____

EXPENSES

HOUSING:

    RENT/MORTGAGE_____ $_____

ASSOCIATION FEES OR DUES_____ $_____

    INSURANCE_____ $_____

    TAXES_____ $_____

    HOME MAINTENANCE_____ $_____

    UTILITIES:

        GAS _____ $_____

        ELECTRICITY_____ $_____

        WATER_____ $_____

        TELEPHONE_____ $_____

        CABLE/INTERNET SERVICE_____ $_____

CREDIT CARD/INSTALLMENT DEBT_____ $_____

STUDENT/EDUCATION LOANS_____ $_____

TRANSPORTATION:

    AUTOMOBILE LOAN/LEASE PAYMENT_____ $_____

    GAS/MAINTENANCE_____ $_____

    INSURANCE_____ $_____

FOOD_____ $_____

MEDICAL_____ $_____

WORK-RELATED EXPENSES _____ $_____

PENSION/401(k) CONTRIBUTION_____ $_____
IRA CONTRIBUTION_____ $_____
SAVINGS_____ $_____
SUPPORT OF DEPENDENT(S)_____ $_____
TAXES:
     PROPERTY TAXES_____ $_____
     INCOME TAXES_____ $_____
CHARITABLE CONTRIBUTIONS_____ $_____
INSURANCE:
     LIFE INSURANCE_____ $_____
     HEALTH INSURANCE_____ $_____
     LONG-TERM CARE INSURANCE_____ $_____
     UMBRELLA LIABILITY INSURANCE_____ $_____
     PROPERTY INSURANCE:_____ $_____
       SCHEDULED PROPERTY_____ $_____
       JEWELRY_____ $_____
PERSONAL EXPENSES:
     CLOTHING_____ $_____
     ENTERTAINMENT_____ $_____
     TRAVEL_____ $_____
     EDUCATION_____ $_____
     GIFTS_____ $_____
     PERSONAL ITEMS_____ $_____
ESTIMATE OF TOTAL MONTHLY EXPENSES_____ $_____
ESTIMATE OF TOTAL ANNUAL EXPENSES _____ $_____

Action Plan

This action plan is a reminder of the information that is important for you to have on hand at any time, especially at the time of the death of a loved one.

1. Review your personal documents and revise them as needed.
   - Statutory Durable Power of Attorney
   - Medical Power of Attorney
   - Living Will/Directives to Physicians
   - Last Will and Testament
   - Trust Agreements
   - Burial Arrangements/Funeral Plans/Obituary Notice

2. Contact the Social Security Administration.
   - Report the death.
   - Request the necessary changes for survivor benefit payments.
   - Apply for the one-time death benefit.
   - Request direct deposit of any social security benefits to your designated checking account.

3. Work with your CPA and attorney to file:
   - Estate Tax Return—due nine months after date of death
   - Federal and State Tax Returns

4. Other contacts:
   - Insurance Companies
     - Request claim forms.
     - File for benefits
     - Request Form 712 (paid insurance claims) for Estate Tax Return.
   - Banks/Credit Unions
     - Report the death.
     - Check for insurance coverage on loans.
   - Current and Former Employers
     - Report the death.
     - Check for potential benefits (group insurance, pension, etc.)
   - Professional, fraternal, other associations
     - Report the death.
     - Cancel publications.

- Request a refund of unused dues.
- Check for assistance or benefits.
- Department of Veterans Affairs in the case of military service.

5. Review your life insurance, property insurance, auto insurance, and liability insurance.
   - Ensure that the ownership of the policy is correct and current.
   - Ensure that the beneficiary designations are current:

6. Consult with a tax professional before making decisions regarding:
   - Joint accounts
   - Titles and deeds to vehicles and/or real estate
   - Retirement and investment accounts

   NOTE: *Ownership changes and asset transfers may have tax implications best evaluated by a tax professional or attorney.*

7. Review your credit card accounts:
   - Pay off and cancel individual store credit cards; use one or two major credit cards for any non-cash purchases.
   - Consolidate multiple card accounts (more than one American Express,
   - MasterCard, Visa) into one card per provider.
   - Change the cardholder name on credit card accounts to you as primary and sole cardholder.
   - Inquire about possible life insurance or accidental death insurance benefits payable through the credit card company.

8. Obtain a copy of your credit report from one of the major credit reporting companies (Equifax, Experian, Transunion).
   - Notify the credit reporting companies of a death. Ensure that the social security number is not being used fraudulently.
   - Consider a credit watch service. You will be notified immediately if there are irregularities on your credit accounts or any unusual activity using your name or social security number.

9. Use the "belt and suspenders" approach to matters of personal safety.
   - Do you have a home fire extinguisher?
     - Where is it?
     - How old is it?
     - Do you know how to use it?

- Multipurpose extinguishers are available in a variety of sizes. Ensure that one is accessible and you know how to activate it. For peace of mind, you may want to have a fire extinguisher in the kitchen, the laundry area, the garage, and your bedroom.
- Does your house have a smoke detector or alarm system?
    - Is it battery-powered?
    - Do you have a regular schedule for changing the batteries?
- Does your house have a carbon monoxide detector or alarm?
    - If not, do you need to consider having one installed?
- Do you have a 24-hour pharmacy?
    - Do you know the telephone number?
    - Is delivery service available?
    - Is there a drive-through window for pick-up?
    - Are you registered at the pharmacy if a physician needs to call in a prescription during the night?
- Do you have a medical condition for which you should wear a medic alert bracelet?
- If you live alone, should you consider having a personal in-home monitoring system?
- If you drive an older car, do you have an extended warranty?
    - Is a roadside assistance service readily available through AAA, an extended warranty plan, automobile dealership, or satellite tracking service such as Onstar?
    - Do you have a cellular phone in the car in the event of an emergency or need? Is it charged? Do you know how to get help if needed?
- Do you have a service warranty for the appliances in your home? (A service warranty—not the same as the manufacturer's warranty for new appliances—covers service calls and repairs to most major appliances.) Repairs can be expensive, unanticipated, unbudgeted costs.

NOTES

Chapter 1: Naming Grief

1. Fanny J. Crosby, "To God Be the Glory" (1875).

2. W. H. Auden, "Funeral Blues," *Another Time* (London: Faber and Faber, 1936), 91.

3. William Shakespeare, *Much Ado About Nothing,* act 3, scene 1.

4. Harold Kushner, interview by Bob Abernethy, *Religion and Ethics News Weekly,* November 26, 2004, http://www.pbs.org/wnet/religionandethics/video/by-faith/christian/feature-psalm-23/958/ (accessed August 9, 2011).

5. Henry Scott Holland, Canon of St. Paul's Cathedral, from a sermon, "The King of Terrors," delivered in St. Paul's Cathedral on May 15, 1910, while the body of King Edward VII was lying in state at Westminster. http://en.wikisource.org/wiki/The_King_of_Terrors (accessed August 9, 2011).

6. Alexander Pope, quoted in S. Austin Allibone, *Prose Quotations from Socrates to Macaulay* (Philadelphia: J.P. Lippincott & Co., 1880), 37.

7. Malcolm Gladwell, *The Tipping Point* (New York: Little, Brown and Company, 2000).

8. Leighton K. Farrell, "Life's Difficulties," sermon preached at Highland Park United Methodist Church, Dallas, Texas, December 27, 1981.

9. Harold Kushner, *When Bad Things Happen to Good People* (New York: Anchor Books, 1982), 140.

10. C.S. Lewis, *A Grief Observed* (San Francisco: HarperCollins, 1961), 3.

11. *The American Heritage® Dictionary of the English Language, Fourth Edition* (Boston: Houghton Mifflin Harcourt, 2006), s.v. "fear."

12. Edmund Burke, *A Philosophical Inquiry into the Origin of Our Ideas of the Sublime and Beautiful* (New York: Oxford University Press, 2008), 53.

13. Leighton K. Farrell, *Cries from the Cross* (Nashville: Abingdon Press, 1994), 46–47.

14. Roget's II: *The New Thesaurus, Third Edition* (Boston: Houston Mifflin Harcourt, 2003), s.v. "suffer."

15. Hans Küng, *On Being a Christian* (Garden City: Doubleday & Company, 1976), 436.

16. *The American Heritage Dictionary of the English Language, Fourth Edition* (Boston: Houghton Mifflin Harcourt, 2006), s.v. "suffer."

17. Doug Manning, *Don't Take My Grief Away: What to Do When you Lose a Loved One* (San Francisco: HarperCollins, 1984), 91.

18. Leighton K. Farrell, "Grief and Death," sermon preached at Highland Park United Methodist Church, Dallas, Texas, February 12, 1995.

19. Leighton K. Farrell, "The Will of God," sermon preached at Highland Park United Methodist Church, Dallas, Texas, September 30, 1984.

Chapter 2: Understanding Grief

1. Elisabeth Kubler-Ross, *On Death and Dying* (New York: Touchstone, 1997).

2. Henry van Dyke, "Time Is," *Music and Other Poems* (New York: Charles Scribner's Sons, 1904), 105.

3. Kathleen Norris, *Dakota: A Spiritual Geography* (Boston: Mariner Books, 2001), 145.

4. Thomas Merton, *Thoughts in Solitude* (New York: Farrar, Straus and Giroux, 1999), 79.

Chapter 3: Yielding to Grief

1. Isaac Watts, "I'll Praise My Maker While I've Breath" (1719).

2. Mitch Albom, "If You Had One Day with Someone Who's Gone..." *Parade*, September 17, 2006.

3. Percy Bysshe Shelley, "To a Skylark," *The Oxford Book of English Verse: 1250–1900* (Oxford: Clarendon, 1919), 702–6.

4. Henri J.M. Nouwen, *The Inner Voice of Love: A Journey Through Anguish to Freedom* (New York: Doubleday, 1999), 34-35.

5. Dag Hammarskjöld, *Markings* (New York: Random House, 2006), 85.

6. John Ness Beck, *"The Quiet Heart"* (Columbus, Ohio: Beckenhorst Press, 1981).

7. Henri Nouwen, *Turn My Mourning Into Dancing* (Nashville: Thomas Nelson, 2001), 76.

8. Eda LeShan quotation, http://www.quoteworld.org/quotes/8214 (accessed August 9, 2011).

9. Paul Tillich, *The Eternal Now* (New York: Charles Scribner's Sons, 1963), 17–18, 21.

10. William Penn, in a 1699 tract written to his children as he prepared for a voyage, quoted in *The Friends' Library,* vol. 5, William Evans and Thomas Evans, eds. (Philadelphia: The Religious Society of Friends, 1841), 299.

11. William Barclay, *The Gospel of John: The New Daily Study Bible,* vol. 2 (Louisville: Westminster John Knox, 2001), 148.

12. Henry L. Carrigan Jr., Editor, *The Temple: The Poetry of George Herbert* (Brewster, Mass.: Paraclete Press, 2001), 8.

13. Nouwen, *Turn My Mourning into Dancing,* 80.

14. Marcus Aurelius quotation, 1-Famous-Quotes.com, Gledhill Enterprises, 2011.http://www.1-famous-quotes.com/quote/547808 (accessed August 9, 2011).

15. Leighton K. Farrell, "Grief and Death," sermon preached at Highland Park United Methodist Church, Dallas, Texas, February 12, 1995.

16. Horatius Bonar, *Hymns of Faith and Hope* (London: James Nesbit, 1861), 52–54.

Chapter 4: Responding to Grief

1. Viktor E. Frankl, *Man's Search for Meaning* (Boston: Beacon Press, 2006), 112–13.

2. Ibid., 146.

3. Leighton K. Farrell, "Grief and Death," sermon preached at Highland Park United Methodist Church, Dallas, Texas, February 12, 1995.

4. George Eliot, *Adam Bede* (Oxford: Oxford University Press, 2008), 435–36.

5. James Allen, *The Life Triumphant: Mastering the Heart and Mind* (Blacksburg: Wilder Publications, 2009), 8.

6. *Roget's II: The New Thesaurus, Third Edition* (Boston: Houston Mifflin Harcourt, 2003), s.v. "victim."

7. Molly Fumia, *Safe Passage* (San Francisco: Conari Press, 2003), 68.

8. Patsy Brundige and Pat Millican, *Hope for a Widow's Shattered World* (Lincoln, Neb.: iUniverse, 2005), 61.

Chapter 5: Adjusting Through Grief

1. See http://www.prb.org/Articles/2001/AroundtheGlobeWomenOutlive-Men.aspx (accessed August 22, 2011).

2. John M. Tyler, *The Whence and the Whither of Man: A Brief History of His Origin and Development Through Conformity to Environment; being the Morse lectures of 1895* (New York: Charles Scribner's Sons, 1899), 212.

3. Eric Hoffer, *The Ordeal of Change* (New York: Harper & Row, 1963), 1.

4. Molly Fumia, *Safe Passage* (York Beach, Main: Conari Press, 2003), 167.

5. Henri J.M. Nouwen, *The Inner Voice of Love: A Journey Through Anguish to Freedom,* (New York, Doubleday, 1998), 34–35.

6. Reinhold Niebuhr, as quoted in Elisabeth Sifton, *The Serenity Prayer: Faith and Politics in Times of Peace and War* (New York: W.W. Norton & Company, 2005), 277.

7. Ashley Davis Prend, *Transcending Loss* (New York: Berkley Publishing Group, 1997), xvi.

Chapter 6: Moving Forward in Grief

1. H. Henry Taylor, *Philip Van Artevelde* (1834), part 1, act 1, scene 5.

2. See "As 9/11 Draws Near, a Debate Rises: How Much Tribute Is Enough?" by N. R. Kleinfield, *New York Times,* September 2, 2007, http://www.nytimes.com/2007/09/02/nyregion/02fatigue.html.

3. Molly Fumia, *Safe Passage* (York Beach, Main: Conari Press, 2003), 114.

4. See http://thesaurus.com/browse/recover (accessed August 9, 2011).

5. Carl P. Daw Jr., "We Come, O Christ" (Pittsburgh: Selah Publishing, 1993), 5–6. http://www.selahpub.com/SelahPDF/420-633-WeComeOChrist.pdf (accessed August 9, 2011).

6. *The American Heritage Dictionary of the English Language, Fourth Edition* (Boston: Houghton Mifflin Harcourt, 2006), s.v. "hap."

7. Elizabeth Gilbert, *Eat, Pray, Love* (New York: Viking Penguin Group, 2006), 260.

8. Joseph Addison, http://thinkexist.com/quotation/three_grand_essentials_to_happiness_in_this_life/148198.html (accessed August 9, 2011).

9. Albert Schweitzer as quoted in David F. Allen, *In Search of the Heart* (McLean, Virginia: Curtain Call Productions, 2004), 174.

10. Robert Lowry, "How Can I Keep from Singing?" *Bright Jewels for the Sunday School* (New York: Biglow and Main, 1869), 16.

11. Oliver Goldsmith, *The Captivity, An Oratorio* (1764), act 2, scene 1.

Chapter 8: Living Beyond Grief

1. Natalie Sleeth, "Hymn of Promise" (Carol Stream, Ill.: Hope Publishing, 1985); as published in *The United Methodist Hymnal* (Nashville: The United Methodist Publishing House, 1989), 707.

2. Leighton K. Farrell, "Grief and Death," sermon preached at Highland Park

United Methodist Church, Dallas, Texas, February 12, 1995.

3. William Barclay, *The Gospel of John: The New Daily Study Bible* (Louisville: Westminster John Knox, 2001), 46.

4. Robert McAfee Brown, as quoted in Molly Fumia, *Safe Passage* (York Beach, Maine: Conari Press, 2003), 245.

5. Elizabeth Barrett Browning, *Sonnets from the Portuguese and Other Love Poems* (Garden City: Doubleday & Company, 1954), 57.

6. Paul Escamilla, *Longing for Enough in a Culture of More* (Nashville, Abingdon Press, 2007), 4–5.

7. Joan Wester Anderson, *Where Angels Walk, True Stories of Heavenly Visitors* (New York: Random House, 1993), 233–34.

8. Margaret A. Farley, "Forms of Faith," *The Living Pulpit* 1:2 (April/June, 1992), 4–5.

SUPPLEMENT
Chapter 9: Grief at the Holidays

1. *The American Heritage Dictionary of the English Language, Fourth Edition* (Boston: Houghton Mifflin Harcourt, 2006), s.v. "dread."

2. Edna St. Vincent Millay, as quoted in Nancy Milford, *Savage Beauty: The Life of Edna St. Vincent Millay* (New York: Random House, 2002), 328.

3. Umphrey Lee, "The Festival of Beginning Again," message to the congregation of Highland Park United Methodist Church, Dallas, Texas, December 23, 1928.

4. Fra Giovanni Giocondo, from a letter written to Countess Allagia Aldobrandeschi on Christmas Eve, 1513, http://www.soberrecovery.com/forums/spirituality/55279-letter-written-fra-giovanni.html (accessed August 9, 2011).

5. Fred Kaan, *A Hymn for Advent* (Carol Stream, Illinois: Hope Publishing, 1975, 1977).